D0128374

Stuart Yarnold

COMPUTER HELP
FOR SENIORS

For the Over 50s

In easy steps is an imprint of Computer Step
Southfield Road · Southam
Warwickshire CV47 0FB · United Kingdom
www.ineasysteps.com

Notice of Liability
Every effort has been made to ensure that this book
contains accurate and current information. However,
Computer Step and the author shall not be liable for
any loss or damage suffered by readers as a result of
any information contained herein.

Trademarks
All trademarks are acknowledged as belonging to their
respective companies.

Printed and bound in the United Kingdom

ISBN-13 978-1-84078-345-2
ISBN-10 1-84078-345-1

Contents

1 Before You Start

Before you start troubleshooting you should be aware of some basic techniques, and know where your computer's various parts are located.

How to Go About It

There are basically two approaches to tackling a problematic computer system:

- You can sit back and ponder what's just happened (or hasn't happened)

- You can get extremely agitated, throw caution to the wind and start frantically clicking buttons and adjusting settings, or worse

Which approach is likely to be the best in terms of finding a solution?

Going at it like a bull in a china shop might, if you're lucky, result in a quick fix. It might also, though, turn a relatively simple problem into a major one.

Spending a few moments in thought before you make your move will undoubtedly increase your chances of making the right move. While it might not be successful, things probably won't be any worse than they were before.

Which approach you take is up to you and also depends on circumstances. For example, you might need the PC urgently and so decide to take a chance, figuring you've nothing to lose as it's not working anyway. On the other hand, you might be one of those who don't use the PC for anything important and know absolutely nothing about them anyway. If so, you might decide to take it down to the local repair shop the next time you're in town.

For a guaranteed fix, the latter is probably the best course of action. However, probably the majority of users will be unable or unwilling to be without their PCs for the length of time this will involve. So what are these people to do?

Many will immediately phone a computer helpline. A lot of these will get good advice and will soon be back bashing their keyboards. Others, however, won't – and will find the experience both frustrating and costly.

Beware

While it would be unfair to tar all computer helplines with the same brush, it is a fact that the advice given by many of them can actually be anything but helpful.

A common problem with helpline operators occurs when they are asked a question to which they do not have an answer. Rather than admit this, they will often advise the caller to reinstall Windows, when in reality the solution may be much simpler.

Common Causes of PC Faults

The only other course of action is to do it yourself. Before you start, though, you should be aware that most faults are user-induced. So it's quite likely that the problem is due to something that you have recently done on the PC.

Therefore, the first thing to do is to think back to what you were doing prior to the fault manifesting itself. If you can identify something specific then very often simply "undoing" it will resolve the problem.

For example, it's extremely likely you have been doing one of the following:

Downloading from the Internet

There are hundreds of thousands of known viruses and more are being developed all the time – the vast majority being spread via the Internet. Many of these viruses can mimic literally any computer fault.

There is also the issue of malware – see page 144. Some of these programs can play havoc with your computer.

So if your PC starts playing up after downloading from the Internet, there is a good chance it has attracted an unwelcome visitor. Obtain up-to-date antivirus and malware detection programs and scan your system with them.

Installing a Hardware Device

Installing and configuring hardware with modern operating systems such as Windows XP and Windows Vista is usually very straightforward. This was not the case with earlier versions of Windows and it often resulted in resource conflicts.

In the unlikely event that you experience problems after installing a device with either of the aforementioned operating systems, uninstall it and see if this resolves the problem. If it does, it is likely that the device simply isn't compatible with the operating system and is causing it (or another device in the system) to malfunction.

Don't forget

Most problems users experience with computers are caused by the users themselves doing things they shouldn't.

Hot tip

If you have problems after an Internet session or opening an email, there is a strong possibility that the computer has picked up a virus or malware.

...cont'd

Beware

Be very wary of installing Shareware and Freeware programs downloaded from the Internet. They often contain an unwelcome attachment.

Visit the manufacturer's website and see if there is an updated driver available for the device, which may enable it to function with the operating system.

Otherwise, you may have to replace the device with one that's compatible.

Installing New Software
Although relatively rare, there are programs that are not compatible with the operating system being used. Uninstall the program and see if the issue is resolved.

You should also be aware that many malware programs are attached to legitimate programs available on the Internet. When the legitimate program is installed so is the malware (without your knowledge). The problem here is that uninstalling the legitimate program will not uninstall the malware. You will also have to run a malware detection program to get rid of it.

Deleting a Program
Often we install a program to try it out and then, having decided we don't want it, uninstall it. With most programs there is no problem.

Hot tip

When uninstalling a program, you may see a message stating that files about to be deleted might be required by other applications and offering you a choice as to whether to keep them or not. Always choose to keep these files just in case they are needed.

However, there are some that simply refuse to go quietly. The usual problem is that these programs "borrow" files already on the system and then, when they are uninstalled, take these files with them. Any other programs on the PC that need the files will then not run correctly, if at all. The fix for this is to reinstall the affected program.

Running a Program
Sometimes, simply running a program will cause problems. This might happen because it has become corrupted or is conflicting with something else on the system.

Most commonly in this situation the PC will either lock up or slow down. Close the program with the Task Manager (see page 176), reboot and then run the program again. In most cases this will resolve the issue.

Changing Your PC's Settings

Windows operating systems offer numerous customizing options, which enable the user to make many changes to the default settings. While most settings relate to a specific function or application, and thus do not have a system-wide effect, there are some that do – registry and BIOS settings in particular.

If you do experience problems after changing a setting, undo the change to resolve the issue. If you can't remember what you did, use System Restore (see page 36) to undo the change.

Shutting Down Your PC Incorrectly

There is a right way and a wrong way to shut down or restart your computer. The right way is to select Start, Restart or Start, Shutdown.

The wrong way is to hit the reset button or the power off button. This can corrupt any program that might be running, including Windows itself. In the case of Windows, it may result in you not being able to get the computer running on restart (we look at this issue in Chapter Three).

Usually, though, the effects are minor and can be repaired by restarting, and then exiting in the proper manner and running Chkdsk (see page 51).

Maintenance/Upgrading

If you have been cleaning the back of the system case, or installing a device inside it, it's quite possible that you have inadvertently loosened or even disconnected something.

Retrace your steps, making sure all boards and cables are firmly seated in their sockets.

Don't forget

Changing a computer's settings without fully understanding the possible consequences is a major cause of so-called faults.

Hot tip

Many problems can be resolved by the simple expedient of rebooting or switching off and then on again. These actions will clear the memory and reset many settings, which might have become misconfigured.

Read the Instructions

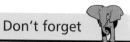

Don't forget

Some applications, video adapter drivers in particular, can cause incompatibility issues with your system. These are often documented in a "Readme" or "Help file" on the installation disc. Make a point of reading these files as doing so can save a lot of time.

Hot tip

Investigating the contents of an installation disc will often reveal the presence of useful applications.

For example, TV tuner installation discs very often contain a free video editing program.

Another frequent cause of problems, usually when installing a new hardware device, is failure to read the installation instructions. Some devices are very simple to install but others require a bit more attention.

For example, it's not uncommon for some devices or programs to be sold with known bugs that can cause incompatibility issues with other hardware or software on the system.

Furthermore, very often these will not be documented in the installation manual but rather in a file on the installation disc entitled "README" or similar. Taking a few minutes to read these instructions can save hours of head-scratching and frustration.

All you have to do is right-click the CD/DVD icon in My Computer and then click Open. This will reveal the contents of the disc.

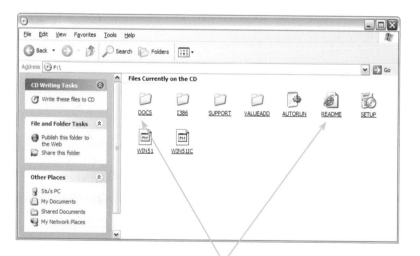

This screenshot, taken from the Windows XP installation CD, shows a README file and also a DOCS folder, both of which contain information relevant to installing XP. How many people have read them, though?

Isolating the Fault

Sometimes you will have absolutely no clues as to what is causing the problem. It will be a head-scratcher knowing even where to begin. It's in situations like this that you'll need to adopt the "sit back and ponder" approach. What you've got to do is to think logically and eliminate as many possibilities as you can.

The first thing to establish is whether the problem is a hardware or a software fault. If there are no clues as to this, either, reboot the PC into Safe Mode (see page 35) and if the fault has now disappeared, the likelihood is that you have a hardware issue. If it hasn't, it will be software-related.

The way to isolate a faulty item of hardware is to disconnect your hardware devices from the system one by one and then run the PC each time to see if removing the device has resolved the issue.

If it has, there is a problem with either the device or its driver. A corrupt driver is the most likely of these, so simply reconnect the device and reinstall the driver. If the fault is still there, the device is faulty and will need to be replaced.

If you have a software fault, the usual suspect is Windows itself. The only type of third-party program that is likely to have a system-wide effect is malware.

Faults with Windows are mostly minor and are rarely more than an irritant. However, when a major fault does develop, such as refusal to start, constant crashes, etc, very often there is more than one possible cause.

While there is a Windows troubleshooting tool (System Configuration Utility) provided with all versions of Windows, which enables the user to isolate faults on a trial and error basis, doing so can be a painstaking and time-consuming procedure. Because of this, the simplest method of repairing Windows XP is just to reinstall it. Windows Vista provides a means of repairing damaged startup files. We look at these procedures in Chapter Three.

Don't forget

The first step is to establish that the fault is either hardware- or software-related. This narrows down the number of possible causes considerably.

13

Don't forget

The simplest way to repair Windows faults is to reinstall the operating system. This replaces any damaged files with good versions.

Hardware Substitution

In Chapter Two, we'll see how to isolate faulty system hardware, e.g. memory, video, etc, with a diagnostic program that produces a series of coded beeps. For example: faulty memory is indicated by continuous beeping, while a faulty video system is indicated by eight beeps.

However, it must be said that this method can sometimes be rather ambiguous. A typical example is when a motherboard is flagged as being faulty when, in fact, it is the CPU (located on the motherboard) that is faulty.

If you didn't know better (and most users don't), you would buy a new motherboard and then take the CPU out of the old board and install it in the new one. This would be a waste of time and money.

In the above scenario, what you should do first is check the CPU, and to do this you need another one of the same type as a substitute for the one in use. This establishes clearly where the fault lies – CPU or motherboard.

The same applies to other system hardware, such as memory, the video card and the monitor. These parts are expensive and you don't want to be shelling out your hard-earned cash unneccessarily – you need to be certain that the part in question is faulty before going out and buying a new one.

The only way to establish this conclusively is to replace the suspect part with one that you know is good. If you don't have a replacement, try making a few phone calls to friends and family. As many people do upgrade their computers and keep the original parts for just this sort of purpose, you may well unearth what you are looking for.

Should you ever decide to upgrade a working device to improve the capabilities of your PC, instead of throwing it away, keep it; you never know when it might come in handy.

Hot tip

Make a point of keeping any working components that you decide to upgrade. Having a supply of usable hardware components is the most useful troubleshooting aid you can have.
    This is what computer repair shops do. Rather than try and find a specific fault on a circuit board or device, they will simply replace it with a working model.

Anatomy of a Computer

If you want to be able to deal with hardware problems, it will help enormously if you have some knowledge of your PC's components and where to find them.

Inside the Computer

Power supply unit   Case fan   CD/DVD drive

Motherboard   Hard drive   Floppy drive (hidden)

...cont'd

At the Back of the Computer

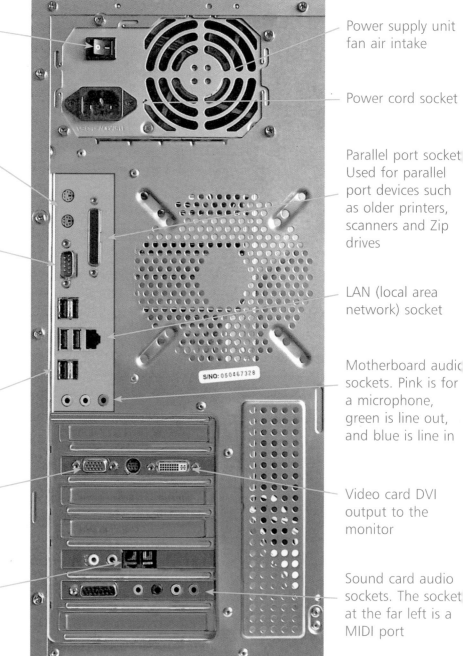

Power supply unit on/off switch

PS/2 ports. The green one is for the mouse, the purple for the keyboard

Serial port. This is obsolete but is provided for backward compatibility

USB ports. USB is the standard type of connection now

Video card VGA output to the monitor

Modem socket for connection to the telephone line

Power supply unit fan air intake

Power cord socket

Parallel port socket Used for parallel port devices such as older printers, scanners and Zip drives

LAN (local area network) socket

Motherboard audio sockets. Pink is for a microphone, green is line out, and blue is line in

Video card DVI output to the monitor

Sound card audio sockets. The socket at the far left is a MIDI port

S/NO: 050467328

The Motherboard

Ports   CPU socket   Memory sockets   ATX power connector   BIOS chip

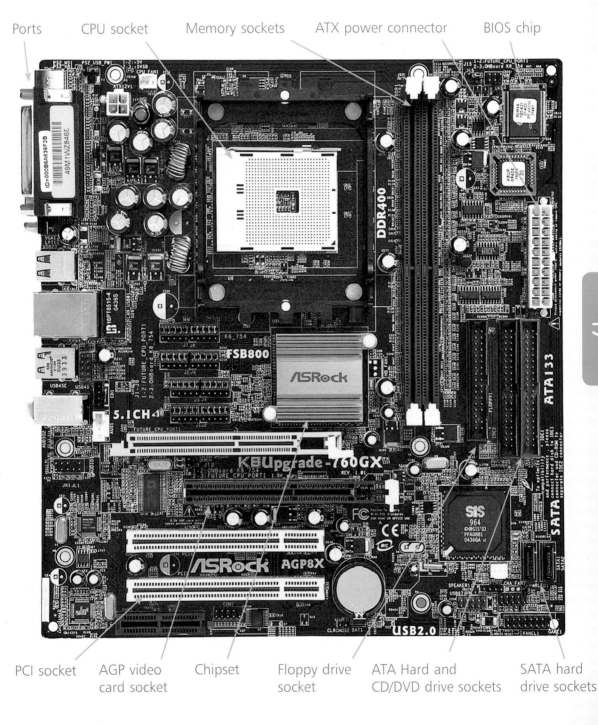

PCI socket   AGP video card socket   Chipset   Floppy drive socket   ATA Hard and CD/DVD drive sockets   SATA hard drive sockets

...cont'd

The Drive Cage
Located at the front of the system case, the drive cage is where the drives in your system are installed.

CD/DVD drive

Floppy drive

Hard drive

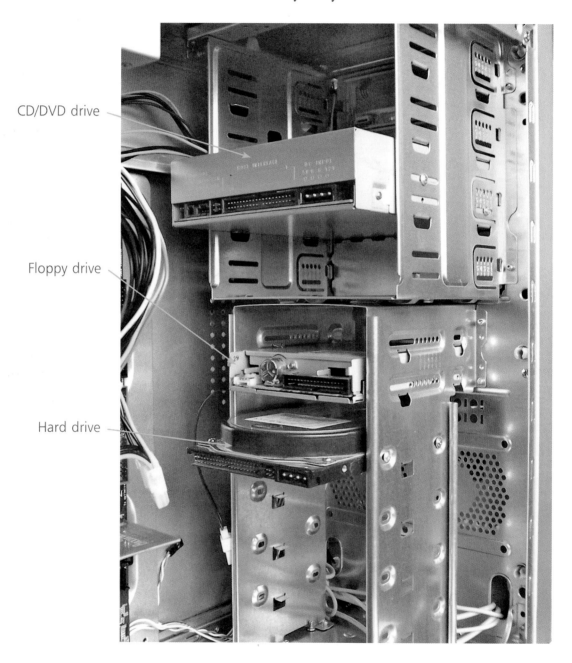

Your Computer's Parts

Motherboard

The motherboard is the large circuit board that you will find screwed to the right-hand side panel of the system case.

This board is such a complex piece of kit that we simply do not have room here to describe it adequately. Suffice to say, essentially, that it is the nervous system of the computer. Every other component, including all the peripheral devices, is connected to it.

Should it ever be necessary to remove the motherboard, this will often require the power supply unit to be removed first and the cables connecting the drive units to be disconnected.

However, as long as you make a note of what goes where, it is a relatively straightforward task to replace one of these boards.

Hot tip

When a motherboard is replaced, some settings in the BIOS may need to be changed depending on what type of hardware is in your system.

Central Processing Unit (CPU)

The CPU is the brains of the computer as it carries out all the calculations, processes instructions and manages the flow of information through the system.

The faster the CPU (these devices are rated in GHz or MHz), the more powerful and capable the PC.

The CPU is located on the motherboard (usually at the top left) and is hidden by a fan/heatsink assembly that prevents it from overheating.

Hot tip

PCs with a slow CPU may struggle to run several programs simultaneously (known as multi-tasking) or a single CPU-intensive application, e.g. video editing.

As with all other parts in the PC, the CPU is easy enough to replace. However, you do need to know what you are doing, so should you decide to attempt it, be sure to read up on the procedure first. ("Building a PC in easy steps" by the same author gives full instructions.)

...cont'd

Memory (RAM)

Memory is a circuit board that contains a number of chips, and is basically an electronic holding place for instructions and data that your computer's CPU can access quickly.

20

When your computer is running, its memory contains the main parts of the operating system and some, or all, of the open applications and related data that are in use.

Memory is an extremely important component and, as with a slow CPU, an insufficient amount (memory is rated in MB) will result in a sluggish PC. Some types of application require an unusually high amount of memory and without it may be impossible to run at all.

A memory module is very easy to replace as it simply plugs into a socket on the motherboard.

Hard Drive

This device is where your data is stored. When you install a program, its data is written to the hard drive. When you create a file, it is written to the hard drive.

You will find it at the front of the system case in the drive cage (usually in the lower half).

There are several different types of hard drive – SCSI, ATA and SATA. However, they all have two connections: a power supply cable from the power supply unit and a data cable to the motherboard.

Replacing a hard drive is not as simple as it may appear at first glance. The physical installation is easy enough – two connections and four securing screws. However, the device also needs to be partitioned and formatted (see page 63) before it can be used.

Video System

Two types of video system are used in PCs: a video card that plugs into the motherboard (shown below) and an integrated video system that is built in to the motherboard.

The video system is responsible for producing the picture that you see on the monitor – without it the monitor would be blank.

Most PCs use integrated video as this is the cheapest option for the manufacturers, and for most purposes it is perfectly adequate. However, integrated video is not as good as a video card, which is essential for some applications, e.g. games and business applications such as Computer Aided Design (CAD).

A video card is also much easier to replace as all you have to do is to unplug it from the motherboard. To replace an integrated system, you will have to replace the motherboard as it is part and parcel of the board.

Hot tip

Should you ever replace a video card, make sure it is compatible with the motherboard. Modern video cards use the PCI-Express connection while older ones use the AGP connection.

...cont'd

Sound System

Sound systems are much the same as video systems in that they come in two types – integrated sound systems and plug-in sound cards. The pros and cons of both types are the same as for the two types of video systems.

CD/DVD Drive

This device serves two purposes:

Don't forget

CD/DVD drives have an internal lens that reads the data on the disc. Over time, this lens can become obscured by grime and, as a result, may have trouble reading the disc.

Typical symptoms of this include the drive taking a long time to read a disc or even the PC locking up.

Before you replace the drive, try cleaning the lens with a lens cleaning disc. They don't always work but it's worth a try.

- It provides a means of importing data to the PC, e.g. installing a program from a CD or DVD

- In the case of writable models, it provides the user with removable data storage options, i.e. you can write data to a disc and store it in a separate place. This provides an ideal means of backing up important data

The difference between CDs and DVDs is essentially the storage capacity of the disc – 700 MB with a CD and 4.5 GB with a standard DVD.

This device is usually located at the top of the drive cage and is very easy to replace. As with the hard drive, there are four securing screws and two connections – power and data. However, there is no need for partitioning and formatting – connect it and it's ready for use.

Floppy Drive

The floppy drive does the same as a writable CD/DVD drive – it provides data input and data storage options. The difference is that floppy disks can only hold 1.44 MB of data and, furthermore, the drive is very slow in operation.

This device, if present, is usually located in the middle of the drive cage – below the CD/DVD drive and above the hard drive. It is replaced in the same way as the CD/DVD drive.

2 Hardware

This chapter looks at PC startup problems. Causes can be both hardware- and software-related. Here, we look at the hardware aspect.

Computer Fails to Start

When a computer fails to boot up, i.e. to start, it can happen in one of two ways:

- The boot procedure fails to start at all – all you see is a blank screen

- The boot procedure starts but fails to complete

In the second scenario, the problem could be either hardware failure (see pages 31–32) or a software issue (see Chapter Three).

In the first scenario, the problem will be a hardware device that is not functioning correctly. However, it doesn't necessarily mean that the device in question is faulty – it could simply be caused by a bad connection somewhere.

Whichever it is, the first step is determining which of the computer's devices has failed. To help users do this, all computers have a diagnostic utility that examines essential hardware when the computer is started and alerts the user when it finds a device that is not working.

It does this in one of two ways: a series of coded beeps, known as beep codes (see page 27) or a text error message on the screen – see bottom margin note.

The diagnostic utility is built in to the system's BIOS. This is a small chip located on the motherboard that handles all the routines necessary to start the computer. These include identification and testing of the computer's hardware, and loading of the operating system.

Knowing what these routines are and the order in which they are carried out can also help in isolating a faulty hardware device.

To begin with, we'll see what to do when faced with a computer on which the boot procedure fails to start. In this situation, the screen will be blank when it is switched on.

Hot tip

If the symptoms indicate hardware failure, don't despair. The problem could well be no more than a loose connection.

24

Don't forget

If a faulty part is discovered before the video system has initialized, you will hear beep codes. If it comes after, you will see a text error message.

The Power Supply

The first thing to find out is whether you have power available to your PC. This principle applies to any item of electronic or electrical equipment, not just computers. For computers it is easily established by observation.

- Are the LEDs (lights) on the system case lit?

- Are the power supply and motherboard fans running? Check by holding your ear to the side of the system case; if either of the fans is running, you'll hear it

- Do you see any lights on your keyboard?

- Does the computer make a beeping sound when it is switched on?

If the answer to any of these questions is yes, then the system's power supply is operational. This narrows the problem to one of four devices – the monitor, the motherboard, the memory or the video system.

If the answer is no, then check the following:

- Is there power at the wall socket? Plug another appliance into it; if that works then the socket is OK

- Are you using a surge suppressor, cable extension or some similar device? If so, try removing or bypassing it and see if that solves the problem

- Next, check the PC's power cable. Try substituting it with the cable from another piece of equipment, such as an electric kettle – these are often the same type

- Most PCs also have an on/off switch at the top-rear of the case. Check that this isn't in the off position

If none of these is causing the problem then the PC's power supply unit is defective and will need replacing.

Hot tip

The first thing to check when your PC appears to be dead is the power supply. Don't forget to check the external (mains) power supply as well.

25

Don't forget

The easiest way to establish that the power supply unit is operational is to check that the fans are running and that the keyboard and system case lights are on.

The Monitor

If the power supply checks out OK, the next thing to investigate is the monitor.

All modern monitors display a message or splash screen of some sort when switched on to indicate that they are functional. (Note that the monitor must be disconnected from the computer for this to work.)

Switch both monitor and computer off and then disconnect the cable from the video socket. If you're not sure which this is, simply follow the cable from the monitor to where it plugs in at the rear of the system case.

Switch the monitor back on (not the computer) and you should now see a message similar to the one below.

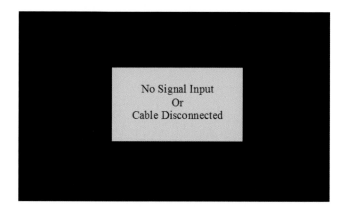

If you don't see a message and the monitor lights are off, then either the monitor itself is faulty or it's not getting any power. Check that there is power at the wall socket; check the power cable, the plug, the fuse and the connections. If these are all OK then the monitor must be faulty.

If you want to be absolutely sure before going out and buying a new monitor, the only conclusive test is to substitute it with one known to be good or connect it to a different system.

Once you have eliminated the monitor, the next thing to check is the motherboard. This takes us into the realm of beep codes.

The Motherboard and CPU

The procedure for eliminating the motherboard from your investigations is simply to listen to the PC in case it is telling you anything in the form of unusual noises when it is switched on. If it is, you will hear an irregular pattern of beeps known as beep codes, which indicate specific faults.

Please note that PCs that use AWARD BIOSs will beep once when switched on. This is normal and indicates that all is well. However, PCs that use AMI BIOSs do not beep when switched on, so if you hear a beep from one you'll know there is a problem.

If you are getting a beep code then you will need to know what the code means. Unfortunately, the different BIOS chip manufacturers all use different codes so first you must find out who the maker of your BIOS is. This information will be in your computer's documentation.

Having established this, look up the code in the table below:

Don't forget

AWARD BIOSs beep once when the PC is started. AMI BIOSs do not – a beep from them indicates a memory problem.

Beeps	Fault
AWARD BIOS	
1 long, 2 short	Video system
Continuous	Memory
1 long, 3 short	Video system
AMI BIOS	
1	Memory
2	Memory
3	Memory
4	Motherboard
5	CPU
6	Motherboard
7	CPU
8	Video system
9 to 11	Motherboard

Hot tip

If your computer uses a BIOS other than the AWARD or AMI versions, you can get details of its beep codes from the manufacturer's website. It will pay you to do this before you have problems with the computer.

...cont'd

If your computer uses an AMI BIOS, four, six, nine, ten or eleven beeps indicate that you have a faulty motherboard. Five or seven beeps indicate a faulty CPU (the CPU is located on the motherboard).

Unfortunately, AWARD BIOSs do not provide beep codes related to motherboard problems. However, if you aren't hearing a code that indicates memory or video problems, and you are sure that the power supply unit and the monitor ore OK, then it is almost certain that the issue is motherboard-related.

Don't forget

If there are no lights on the keyboard when the computer is switched on, this indicates a faulty motherboard.

A further clue is provided by the keyboard LEDs. If these come on when the PC is started, it indicates that the motherboard is active, in which case the problem is more likely to be with the CPU. If they don't, the board is definitely faulty.

Having established that the problem is either the CPU or the motherboard, you either take the computer to a repair shop or replace the faulty part yourself. The latter option is not nearly as difficult as many people imagine and is certainly much quicker (and cheaper) than having it done by someone else.

However, it does require a knowledge of computers that most people don't have. The way round this is to buy one of the self-help books, such as "Building a PC in easy steps" by the author of this book. These will guide you through all the steps necessary to replace any part of the computer.

Something else you should consider if it becomes necessary to replace your motherboard is whether to take the opportunity to upgrade it to a newer and more capable model. However, you should be aware that if you do this, you may also have to upgrade the CPU and memory modules as current models may not be compatible with older motherboards.

Again, should you be uncertain about this, buy a book that gives you all the information you will need.

The Video System

To be able to display text and images on the monitor, the computer must have a functional video system. These come in two versions:

- Integrated video, which is built into the motherboard

- A dedicated video card, which plugs in to the motherboard

If you see text on the screen, you know the video system is working. If you don't, and you have already established that the power supply, monitor, motherboard and CPU are OK, the video system is the part most likely to be causing the problem.

In the case of a PC with an AWARD BIOS, this will be confirmed by a beep code of one long and two short, or one long and three short. With an AMI BIOS, you will get eight beeps.

If your PC uses an integrated video system, as most PCs do, failure of the video system means that you will have to replace the motherboard as it is part and parcel of the board.

In the case of a video card, check the connections before condemning the card. Check that the video cable is securely connected to the card's output socket. Then open the case and reseat the card in the motherboard, making sure it is pushed home completely (they can work loose over time).

If you still have no video then the card itself is faulty and you will have to replace it. However, before you do, it is worth checking that your motherboard doesn't offer an integrated video system (this information will be in the PC's documentation).

If it does, you can switch to it simply by disconnecting the video cable from the video card and connecting it to the motherboard's integrated video system. Not only will this get you back in business, it will also confirm conclusively that the video card is faulty.

Memory

The final hardware device that can be the cause of a PC refusing to boot at all is the memory.

If this is the case, with an AWARD BIOS you will hear a continuous beeping, and with an AMI BIOS, one, two or three beeps.

All you can do in this situation is one of the following:

- Check that the memory module is securely connected. Do this by opening the plastic retaining clips on either side of the memory socket to release the module. Pull it out and then reinsert it. The clips should close automatically

- Remove the module as described above and install it into a different socket; it isn't unheard-of for a memory socket to be faulty

Beware

Of all the parts in a PC that can be damaged by careless handling, memory modules are the most susceptible. You must ground yourself before handling these devices (see page 20).

Module retaining clips. Ensure that the module is handled as little as possible – see margin note

If the problem is still unresolved, the module is faulty and will have to be replaced.

Computer doesn't Start Completely

Referring back to page 24 for a moment, we saw there that another type of boot problem is where the procedure starts but fails to finish.

This is the more likely of the two scenarios, which is fortunate as it is also, usually, the less serious. In this situation you will see text on the screen as the PC starts to boot. This indicates that the motherboard, video system and monitor are all functioning correctly.

The only two hardware devices that can cause the boot procedure to stop once started are the memory and the hard drive. However, software failure (operating system or a device driver – see margin note) can also cause this problem. We'll look at the hardware aspect first, though.

Memory

This is simple to diagnose. Part of the BIOS's startup routine is the memory test or count. This establishes how much memory is installed in the computer. If bootup stops at this point, as shown below, the only possible cause is a faulty memory module. Remove the module and replace it with a new one.

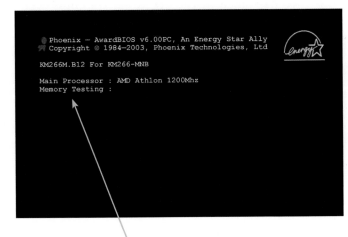

Bootup has stopped at the memory test

...cont'd

Hard Drive

Another part of the BIOS's startup routine is detection and configuration of the hard drive. If the BIOS does not detect a hard drive, or is unable to configure it for some reason, it will halt the boot procedure at the point shown below:

Don't forget

Most hard drive issues are caused by poor connections. This is the first thing to check.

```
  Phoenix — AwardBIOS v6.00PC, An Energy Star Ally
  Copyright © 1984–2003, Phoenix Technologies, Ltd

KM266M.B12 For KM266-MNB

Main Processor : AMD Athlon 1200Mhz
Memory Testing : 262144K OK

    Primary Master :
```

This indicates that the hard drive has either failed or has a connection problem. As out-of-the-blue drive failure is very rare, in most cases the problem is a connection issue. To resolve this, open the system case and reseat the drive cable connections both to the drive itself and to the motherboard. Do the same with the drive's power plug connection. In the unlikely event that this doesn't fix the problem, you have a drive that has failed and that will need to be replaced.

If you see the error message shown below (or similar), either the hard drive has failed or the operating system is damaged.

Hot tip

Modern hard drives are extremely reliable devices and, in any case, will almost always give plenty of advance warning of impending failure.

```
Verifying DMI Pool Data…
Boot From CD:

Disk Boot Failure, Insert System Disk and Press Enter
```

First, check the hard drive as described above and if the problem is still unresolved, check the operating system as described in Chapter Three.

3 Software

This chapter shows how to get both Windows XP and Windows Vista running in the event of either failing to start.

Windows won't Start

In Chapter Two we saw that one of the causes of PCs refusing to start is faulty hardware. In this chapter we look at the other cause – software corruption. This can be in Windows itself, the file system or a hardware driver.

When this happens, the boot procedure will get to a certain point and then stop. You may get an error message or just a blank screen. No matter how many times you try, the result is the same.

The most common cause of this is exiting Windows incorrectly.

34

Instead of clicking Turn Off or Restart, you may have done one of the following:

- Pressed the PC's reset button

- Switched the computer off with the on/off button while Windows was running

- Crashed the computer

With any of these "exits" you run the risk of corrupting operating system startup files or creating file system errors with the result that Windows may refuse to load on restart.

The first thing to check is the possibility of file system corruption and to do this you need to get back into Windows to run the disk checking utility Chkdsk.

The question is, how can you do it if you can't get into Windows in the first place?

Safe Mode

The answer is to start Windows in Safe Mode – see margin note. This is the Windows troubleshooting mode and is designed to get the system going if at all possible.

To do it, reboot and keep tapping the F8 key until you see the Windows Advanced Options menu. Using the arrow keys, scroll to Safe Mode and press Enter.

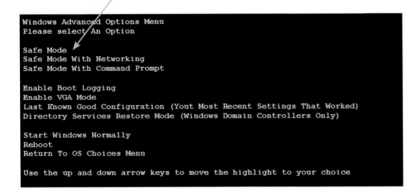

```
Windows Advanced Options Menu
Please select An Option

Safe Mode
Safe Mode With Networking
Safe Mode With Command Prompt

Enable Boot Logging
Enable VGA Mode
Last Known Good Configuration (Yout Most Recent Settings That Worked)
Directory Services Restore Mode (Windows Domain Controllers Only)

Start Windows Normally
Reboot
Return To OS Choices Menu

Use the up and down arrow keys to move the highlight to your choice
```

Windows should now start. It will take longer than normal so give it time. You will also find that while in Safe Mode, it will run a lot slower and many of its functions will be disabled.

When Windows is running, go to My Computer and right-click the hard drive icon. Click Properties and then open the Tools tab. Under Error-checking, click the Check Now... button. In the dialog box that opens, click Start. You will now get a message saying that the disk cannot be checked while it is in use. Click "Schedule disk check" and then click OK.

Reboot the PC, and just before the point when Windows usually loads, Chkdsk will run and will check the hard drive for file system errors. If it finds any, it will repair them automatically. The PC will then reboot automatically and this time Windows should load OK.

The procedure for starting in Safe Mode is the same whether you are running Windows Vista or XP.

Hot tip

Safe Mode works by bypassing the normal Windows configuration, and instead loading a minimum set of basic drivers. This eliminates a number of issues that might prevent Windows from starting and will usually get you back into Windows from where you can find and fix the problem.

System Restore

Hot tip

Any little niggling problems that Windows develops can be repaired by restoring the system to a restore point made prior to the problem manifesting itself.

Don't forget

Drivers are well known for becoming corrupted (damaged), and when they do they can be the cause of all sorts of problems.

Hot tip

System Restore works by automatically making backups of the system at certain points, e.g. when a program or hardware device is installed. When a fault needs to be corrected, these backups are used to restore the system.

If running Chkdsk fails to resolve the problem, then either Windows or a hardware driver is damaged. Of the two, a hardware driver is the more likely so we'll look at this first.

The usual method of repairing a corrupt driver is just to reinstall it, which is simple enough if you can access Windows. However, if you can't, you have to do it another way – instead of reinstalling the driver, you restore it to its original (working) state.

This procedure involves the System Restore utility (see bottom margin note). Do it as follows:

1 Reboot the PC into Safe Mode

2 When Windows is running, go to Start, All Programs, Accessories, System Tools, System Restore

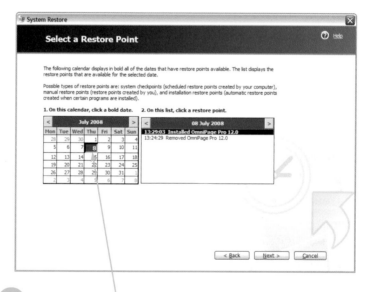

3 Choose a restore point made on a day when the PC was known to be working

The PC (including its drivers) will now be restored to the state it was in when the restore point was made.

Repairing Windows XP

If System Restore doesn't resolve the issue then you almost certainly have a corrupt Windows installation. Also, if you have attempted the procedures described on pages 35 and 36 but were unable to get the PC running in Safe Mode, or to access System Restore, again the cause will be damage to Windows.

What you do depends on which version of Windows you are running – XP or Vista.

To repair Windows XP, you will need the installation disc. However, before you can use it, the PC needs to be configured to boot from the CD/DVD drive (instead of the hard drive, which is the usual arrangement). Do this as follows:

1 Reboot and go into the BIOS setup program (see top margin note). Use the arrow keys to select Advanced BIOS Features and then scroll down to First Boot Device

```
              Phoenix - AwardBIOS CMOS Setup Utility
                      Advanced BIOS Features

  Virus Warning              [Disabled]          Item Help
  CPU Internal Cache         [Enabled]
  External Cache             [Enabled]
  CPU L2 Cache ECC Checking  [Enabled]          Menu Level
  Quick Power On Self Test   [Enabled]
  First Boot Device          [CDROM]            Select Your
  Second Boot Device         [HDD-0]            Boot Device
  Third Boot Device          [Floppy]           Priority
  Boot Other Device          [Enabled]
  Swap Floppy Drive          [Disabled]
  Boot Up Floppy Seek        [Enabled]
  Boot Up NumLock Status     [On]
  Gate A20 Option            [Fast]
  Typematic Rate Setting     [Disabled]
x Typematic Rate (Chars/Sec)  6
x Typematic Delay (Msec)      250
  Security Option            [Setup]
  OS Select For DRAM > 64MB  [Non-OS2]
  HDD S.M.A.R.T. Capability  [Enabled]

  Enter:Select  +/-/PU/PD:Value  F10:Save ESC:Exit  F1:General Help
  F5: Previous Values  F6: Fail-Safe Defaults  F7: Optimized Defaults
```

2 Using the Page Up/Page Down keys, select CDROM. Save your changes (see margin note) and exit the BIOS

Hot tip

To enter the BIOS setup program, reboot the PC and press the appropriate key (see the PC's documentation) as the PC starts.

Don't forget

The tools necessary to repair Windows are on the installation disc. To be able to access them, the PC must be set to boot from the CD/DVD drive.

37

Don't forget

When making a change in the BIOS you must save it before exiting the program, otherwise the change will not be effective. The option to do this is on the main BIOS page.

...cont'd

Now place the installation disc in the CD/DVD drive and boot the computer. After a few moments you will see a message saying "Press any key to boot from CD..." Do so and XP's installation routine will begin.

1 At the first screen, select the first option – set up Windows XP

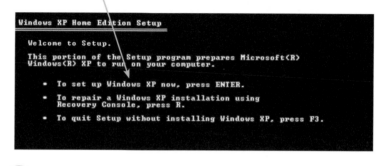

2 At the second screen, choose to repair the existing XP installation by pressing R

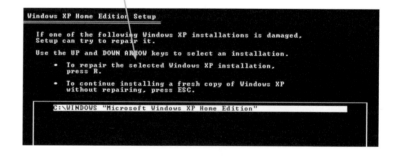

The XP installation will now be repaired. Note that all your data, applications and settings will remain as they were before, so you needn't worry about losing any data.

However, if there is no operating system listed (highlighted in white) as shown in step two above, or you don't see the repair option in step one then the XP installation is damaged beyond repair.

In this case, the only course of action is to do a new installation of Windows XP. Do this as follows:

...cont'd

1 Set the PC to boot from the CD/DVD drive as described on page 37. Then place the XP CD in the CD/DVD drive and boot the PC

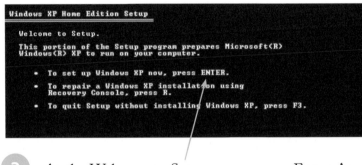

```
Windows XP Home Edition Setup

  Welcome to Setup.
  This portion of the Setup program prepares Microsoft(R)
  Windows(R) XP to run on your computer.

    • To set up Windows XP now, press ENTER.
    • To repair a Windows XP installation using
      Recovery Console, press R.
    • To quit Setup without installing Windows XP, press F3.
```

2 At the Welcome to Setup screen, press Enter. At the next screen, press C to create a partition – see bottom margin note

```
Windows XP Home Edition Setup

  The following list shows the existing partitions and
  unpartitioned space on this computer.

  Use the UP and DOWN ARROW keys to select an item in the list.

    • To set up Windows XP on the selected item, press ENTER.
    • To create a partition in the unpartitioned space, press C.
    • To delete the selected partition, press D.

  4095 MB Disk 0 at Id 0 on bus 0 on atapi [MBR]
      Unpartitioned space              4095 MB
```

3 The next screen allows you to choose the partition size. By default, XP chooses the maximum size

```
Windows XP Home Edition Setup

  You asked Setup to create a new partition on
  4095 MB Disk 0 at Id 0 on bus 0 on atapi [MBR].

    • To create the new partition, enter a size below and
      press ENTER.
    • To go back to the previous screen without creating
      the partition, press ESC.

  The minimum size for the new partition is        8 megabytes (MB).
  The maximum size for the new partition is     4087 megabytes (MB).
  Create partition of size (in MB): 4087
```

Beware

A new installation of Windows involves reformatting the hard drive. This action wipes it clean of all its data, so you must first make a separate backup of all the data you wish to keep.

When the procedure is complete, you will need to reinstall all your programs and backed-up data.

Hot tip

If a partition already exists, you can skip steps 2 and 3. Go to step 4 (shown on the next page).

4 At the next screen, press Enter to set up XP on the selected partition

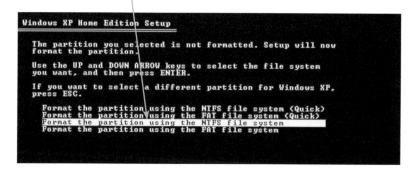

```
Windows XP Home Edition Setup

    The following list shows the existing partitions and
    unpartitioned space on this computer.

    Use the UP and DOWN ARROW keys to select an item in the list.

    •   To set up Windows XP on the selected item, press ENTER.
    •   To create a partition in the unpartitioned space, press C.
    •   To delete the selected partition, press D.

    4095 MB Disk 0 at Id 0 on bus 0 on atapi [MBR]

       C:  Partition1 [New (Raw)]                4087 MB (   4086 MB free)
           Unpartitioned space                      8 MB
```

5 Finally, you will see the Format screen. Make your choice – see margin note – and then press Enter

```
Windows XP Home Edition Setup

    The partition you selected is not formatted. Setup will now
    format the partition.

    Use the UP and DOWN ARROW keys to select the file system
    you want, and then press ENTER.

    If you want to select a different partition for Windows XP,
    press ESC.

       Format the partition using the NTFS file system (Quick)
       Format the partition using the FAT file system (Quick)
       Format the partition using the NTFS file system
       Format the partition using the FAT file system
```

XP will now format the partition. When this is complete, the Windows installation will automatically begin. Simply follow the prompts until the procedure is finished.

When you have the new copy of Windows running, you will have to reinstall all the drivers for your hardware devices from the relevant installation discs, then your programs, and finally all the data from your backups.

Repairing Windows Vista

Vista offers users more options with which to repair a faulty installation. As with XP, the PC must be set to boot from the CD/DVD drive as explained on page 37.

Then boot the PC from the installation disc and when you see the message "Press any key to boot from CD...", do so.

1 At the first screen click Next, and at the following screen click "Repair your computer"

2 Click Startup Repair at the System Recovery Options screen

Hot tip

If your Vista installation is severely damaged it is possible that you won't see the System Recovery Options screen as shown left.

Instead, you will almost certainly get an error message that says no operating system has been found.

In this situation, you will have to reinstall Vista as described on pages 42 and 43.

...cont'd

Vista will now check its startup files, which are the most likely cause of the problem, and if they are damaged it will replace them from the installation disc. The PC will then automatically reboot and all should now be well.

If the PC still refuses to boot up, however, then the Vista installation is seriously damaged and you will need to reinstall it. Do this as follows:

Don't forget

In most cases, failure of a Windows operating system is due to corrupt startup files. Unlike Windows XP, Vista offers a repair option for this scenario.

1   Place Vista's installation disc in the CD/DVD drive and boot the PC. When you see the message "Press any key to boot from CD...", do so. Click Next at the first screen and then click "Install now" at the second screen

Hot tip

You cannot reinstall Vista over an existing copy from the installation disc. The only option offered is to install a new copy.

2   At the next screen, enter the serial number (you'll find this on the installation disc packaging)

3   OK the license agreement, and at the Installation Options screen select Custom (advanced)

4 At the "Where do you want to install Windows?" screen, click Next

Install Windows

Where do you want to install Windows?

Name	Total Size	Free Space	Type
Disk 0 Partition 1	98.2 GB	91.2 GB	Primary

⟳ Refresh   Drive options (advanced)

🔧 Load Driver

Next

Install Windows

Where do you want to install Windows?

Name	Total Size	Free Space	Type
Disk 0 Partition 1	98.2 GB	91.2 GB	Primary

Install Windows

The partition you selected might contain files from a previous Windows installation. If it does, these files and folders will be moved to a folder named Windows.old. You will be able to access the information in Windows.old, but you will not be able to use your previous version of Windows.

OK   Cancel

⟳ Ref

🔧 Loa

Next

Hot tip

This procedure installs a second copy of Vista, which is the one the PC will use. The original copy will be placed in a folder named Windows Old. You can recover your data from this folder but will not be able to use any programs installed on it. These will need to be reinstalled on the new copy.

43

5 Dismiss the warning message by clicking OK, and a new copy of Vista will now be installed. Simply follow the prompts until the procedure is complete.

Restoring Vista from a Backup

Rather than repairing a damaged Windows installation, users of Vista have another option that allows them quickly to replace it with a good copy.

This is available at the System Recovery Options screen (see page 41). However, before you can use it, you must first have created a complete system backup.

It is entirely up to you whether or not you do this, but as it only takes a few minutes and provides you with a guaranteed method of quickly restoring your system, we highly recommend that you do, as described below.

Don't forget

The only caveat with Complete PC Restore is that the backup must be created on a separate hard drive, partition or recordable disc.

Beware

If you restore your system with Complete PC Restore, you will lose all programs installed, and all data and settings created after the backup was made.

To avoid this, we suggest you make a new backup every time you install a new program (the new backup will simply overwrite the old one).

1. Go to Start, All Programs, Accessories, System Tools and click Backup Status and Configuration

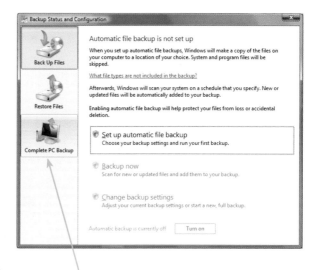

2. Click Complete PC Backup and follow the prompts to create a backup of your system

Having done so, should you ever have a catastrophic failure of Windows, you can use the backup to restore the PC to the state it was in when the backup was made. Do it as described on page 41, but instead of selecting Startup Repair, select Windows Complete PC Restore. Then simply follow the prompts.

4 Performance

In this chapter we look at factors that can cause a PC to underperform. We explain what can be done about them and also show you some tips that will boost your PC's performance.

Check Your Hardware

Before you attempt to improve the performance of your PC, check that it is capable of good performance to begin with.

The hardware components that have the most impact on performance are the Central Processing Unit (CPU) and the memory (RAM). If you are running Windows Vista, the video system is also important.

So what do you need? We'll take a look at the requirements for Vista as this is the latest operating system, and also the most demanding of all in terms of hardware requirements.

The minimum required to run Vista is a CPU rated at a speed of 800 MHz, 512 MB of memory, and a DirectX 9 capable video system. However, while it may run, it won't do so particularly well.

To get good performance from Vista, you will need a CPU of at least 2.0 GHz, 1 GB of memory and a modern video system with at least 128 MB of integral memory that is capable of supporting DirectX 9.

So how do you know what lies under the bonnet of your PC? Details of the CPU, the memory and the video system can be obtained from the System Information utility.

Click Start, All Programs, Accessories, System Tools, System Information.

Hot tip

Older PCs that use an integrated video system, or a low-end video card, will be restricted to the Vista Basic interface. Owners of these computers who wish to run the Aero interface will need to upgrade their video systems.

46

Hot tip

The System Information utility tells you a lot of other things about your system as well.

On the system information page, look down the Item column.

Next to Processor and Total Physical Memory are details of the CPU and memory respectively.

Next, click the Components category on the left and then click Display. In the Item column, next to Adaptor RAM are details of the video system's integral memory capacity.

To find out the version of DirectX installed on your PC, type Dxdiag.exe in the Run box on the Start Menu. (Vista users can also enter this in the Start Menu search box.)

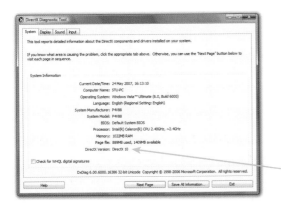

Then press Enter to open the DirectX utility. The version installed is shown here.

Vista users also have a simpler way of evaluating their system's hardware. Go to Start, Control Panel and click Performance Information and Tools.

For general PC use (word processing, Internet, etc), a subscore of two or above is adequate

For graphic-intensive applications, such as PC games and video editing, a rating of three to four will be required.

If the rating of any individual component is less than two, you should upgrade it with a more capable model.

This utility shows the major parts in your PC together with a performance rating (under the Subscore column) – see margin note.

Defragment the Hard Drive

Fragmentation is a term used to describe the way that files saved to a magnetic disk drive have their data split up on different parts of the disk, or disks, instead of being stored contiguously. When a fragmented file is accessed the drive's read/write heads have to hunt about to locate all the different parts of it before they can be reassembled in the original form. The result is that the file will take much longer to open than it should do, and the system will consequently be sluggish.

To address this issue, Windows provides a tool called Disk Defragmenter. This application "undoes" the fragmentation by rearranging the data on the disk so that each file is stored as a complete unit.

Users of Windows Vista do not have to concern themselves about this issue as the defragmentation utility is enabled by default and will automatically defragment the hard drive on a weekly basis.

1 Go to Start, All Programs, Accessories, System Tools

2 Select the hard drive and click Defragment

It is good practice to defragment your hard drive about once a month.

It is very important that you do this, as a severely defragmented drive will affect the performance of a PC drastically.

Program Overload

The next thing to look at is the number of programs you have installed. The more there are, the slower your PC is going to be, even if they are not being used. If this puzzles you, be aware that some types of application (or parts of them) run in the background even if they appear to be closed.

A typical example is a CD/DVD authoring program: these usually install a virtual CD driver that runs even when the program is closed. Many other programs do the same sort of thing.

So the more software you install, inevitably the more of these background applications there will be. Not only do they slow system performance, they also affect shutdown and startup speeds.

The solution is to go through your hard drive and uninstall all programs that you don't need – if you're like most people, there will probably be dozens of them. Windows Vista users can do this as follows:

1 Click Start, Control Panel, Programs and Features

2 Here you will see a list of all the programs that have been installed on the computer

Go through the list and uninstall all the ones you can live without. The more you can get rid of, the better the overall performance of your PC will be.

Resource-Hungry Programs

Certain types of application are well known for having a major impact on a PC's performance. Antivirus and system utility programs are two of the worst offenders.

To be effective, antivirus programs must monitor much of what's going on in the PC and so, inevitably, they slow the system down by a considerable degree. Probably most users consider this to be a price worth paying in order to keep their systems clean.

However, it is a fact that you only need to have an antivirus program running for the following activities:

- When you are connected to the Internet
- When you are opening an email (online or offline)
- When a removable disk (floppy, CD or DVD) is opened
- When a drive is added to the system

These are the ways that viruses get on to a user's PC. If you are connected to the Internet, even if you aren't using it, you must have an antivirus program running. The same applies when opening emails. However, if you aren't doing any of the above, you can safely close your antivirus program. Doing so will give your system a noticeable boost in speed.

With regard to system utilities (an example being Norton System Works), many people use these to maintain their systems. They offer various functions to the user – diagnostics, repair, system tuning, maintenance, etc. Many of these tools can be run as needed and then turned off when finished with, which is fine. Others, however, such as disk monitoring tools that run permanently in the background, can be a real drain on resources and will make a serious hit on the PC's performance.

Our advice is not to use this type of program at all, as Windows supplies you with all the tools you need to keep your system in good shape. If you must use them, at least avoid the monitoring applications and, instead, just use those that can be run when needed and then turned off.

Hot tip

We are not suggesting that you don't need antivirus software. We are just highlighting situations in which it is not necessary.

Hot tip

Many of the tools provided by utility programs are superior to the tools bundled with Windows. Use these by all means; just avoid the system and hard drive monitoring tools that run permanently in the background.

Keep the File System Healthy

Over time, especially if the PC is well used, file system and data faults can build up on the hard drive. Not only can these have an adverse effect on the PC's performance, they can also be the cause of general system instability, and thus potential loss of data.

To correct these types of fault, Windows provides a disk checking utility called Chkdsk.

 Open My Computer and right-click the hard drive. Click Properties and then the Tools tab

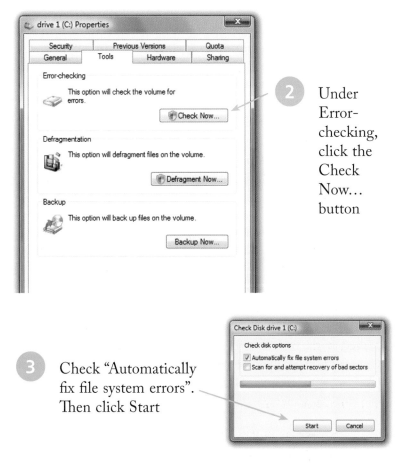

② Under Error-checking, click the Check Now... button

③ Check "Automatically fix file system errors". Then click Start

Note that running Chkdsk on the drive on which Windows is installed will require a system reboot. With all other drives, the procedure is done while Windows is running.

Streamline the Registry

The registry is a central database that holds all the important Windows settings regarding software, hardware, and system configuration. It also provides a common location where all applications can save their launching parameters and data.

Over time, as the user installs and deletes programs, creates shortcuts and changes system settings, etc, obsolete and invalid information builds up in the registry. While this does not have a major impact on a PC's performance, it can be the cause of system and program errors that can lead to instability issues.

The solution is to scan the registry periodically with a suitable application that will locate all the invalid entries and delete them.

While Windows Registry Editor is adequate for editing purposes, it does not provide a cleaning option. However, there are many of these applications available for download from the Internet. A typical example is Registry Mechanic (shown below). These programs provide various options, such as full or selective scans, backups, the creation of System Restore points, etc.

Beware

Changes to the registry can be dangerous. So create a system restore point using System Restore first. If you have any problems as a result of the change, you will be able to undo it by restoring the system.

Hot tip

We recommend you clean the registry about once a month. However, if you frequently install and uninstall software, change system settings, etc, it will be worth doing it more often.

Occasional use of a registry cleaner will help to keep your system stable, and thus more reliable.

Reduce the Visual Effects

Windows comes with a number of visual effects, e.g. fading or sliding menus, drop shadows, pointer shadows, etc. These are all designed to improve the look and feel of the Windows interface. However, they add nothing to its functionality. In fact they can, and do, have a negative impact on the system. Remember: each of these effects consumes system resources.

Users interested in, or needing, performance rather than appearance will benefit from disabling some, or even all, of these essentially unnecessary graphic enhancements. If you are using Vista, do the following:

Click Start, Control Panel, System, Advanced system settings. Then click the Settings button under Performance.

On the Visual Effects tab you will see a list of all Vista's visual effects, plus several user options. By default, Vista chooses the first option and invariably enables the majority, if not all, of the effects.

To disable an effect just uncheck its box. The question is, though, which ones do you disable?

The effects that have the greatest impact on performance are:
- Show shadows under menus
- Use a background image for each folder type
- Use visual styles on windows and buttons
- Use drop shadows for icon labels on the Desktop
- Show thumbnails instead of icons

For maximum performance gain, disable all the effects. Otherwise, disable just the ones in the list above.

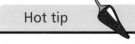

Hot tip

If you are using Windows XP, go to Start, Control Panel, System. Click the Advanced tab and then Settings under Performance.

53

Beware

Disabling all of the effects will have a significant impact on the appearance of Windows.

ReadyBoost

This procedure applies to users of Windows Vista only.

If Vista were to run out of memory the PC would literally grind to a halt. To prevent this, it uses a paging file on the hard drive as a memory substitute. The problem with this, as hard drives are much slower than memory, is that performance is reduced when the paging file is being used.

The solution is to prevent Vista having to use the paging file, and the way to do this is to install more memory. However, many users don't know how to do this; plus, it is expensive.

ReadyBoost provides a simple, and cheaper, alternative. All you need is a USB 2 flash drive with a capacity of between 256 MB and 4 GB. Plug the drive into a spare USB port and the following window will pop up:

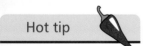
54

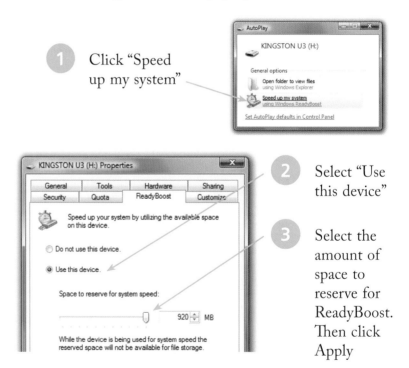

1 Click "Speed up my system"

2 Select "Use this device"

3 Select the amount of space to reserve for ReadyBoost. Then click Apply

Vista will now use the flash drive (which is faster that the hard drive) as a cache for the most commonly paged data, giving your system a noticeable boost in speed. The paging file will still be on the hard drive but will be used much less.

The PC is Slow to Start

This is a common problem that is often caused by simply having too much software installed on the PC – see page 49. Another cause is having a number of programs that automatically start with Windows so that they are open and ready to use when, or shortly after, the Desktop appears.

These programs are located in the Startup folder: they can be placed here by the user if he or she wants them to open with Windows. Also, some programs will automatically place a link here (without the user's knowledge) when they are installed.

As each of these programs must be loaded before Windows is ready for use, the more there are in the Startup folder, the longer startup will take. Check it out as follows:

see page 49

Beware

The more programs you have in your Startup folder, the longer the PC will take to start.

1 Click Start, All Programs, Startup

Hot tip

Another way of finding out which programs are in the Startup folder is via the System Information utility. This is accessible from Start, All Programs, Accessories, System Tools.

2 Here, you'll see a list of applications that start with Windows. Remove any that you don't need by right-clicking and then clicking Delete

...cont'd

However, clearing out the Startup folder is only half the battle. You now have to find and get rid of the startup programs that run unseen in the background, and thus aren't so obvious.

Hot tip

The System Configuration Utility is useful in more ways than one. Among other things, it allows you to view and stop the services running on your PC, troubleshoot boot problems, and launch various Windows tools.

1 Type msconfig in the Start menu's search box and press Enter. This opens the System Configuration utility. Click the Startup tab

![System Configuration dialog box showing the Startup tab with a list of startup items including Windows Defender, NVIDIA Compatible Windows 2000 Displa..., NVIDIA Media Center Library, Update Detection Module, Microsoft Windows Operating System, Microsoft Office OneNote, Mixer, InstantTray, InstantWrite, and PinnacleDriverCheck, with columns for Startup Item, Manufacturer, Command, Location, and Date Disabled. Buttons: Enable all, Disable all, OK, Cancel, Apply, Help]

2 Here you will see a list of more programs that start with Windows

Hot tip

If you want more information on any of the programs (it's not always obvious what they are or do), go to www.sysinfo.org. Here, you will find a huge list of applications that start with Windows, together with explanatory notes.

To disable a program, simply uncheck it. You can, in fact, quite safely disable all of them by clicking the Disable All button – none of them plays any critical role (if they did, there wouldn't be a Disable All button).

However, we would suggest that you refrain from disabling your antivirus program, which will be listed here (assuming you have one). This application plays an essential role in keeping your system free of viruses.

5 Installation/Setting Up

Here, we look at problems associated with the installation of both software and hardware devices.

A Program won't Install

Installing a program is usually very simple – insert the installation disc in the CD/DVD drive and an installation options screen will appear, as shown in the example below.

Hot tip

Alternatively, you can click Open in step two to reveal the contents of the installation disc. Then click the file named Install or Setup.

However, for a number of reasons this may not always happen. With no installation screen, how do you install the program? The solution is as follows:

1   Go to Start, My Computer

2   Right-click the CD/DVD drive and click "Install or run program"

A Program won't Run

When you install programs on your XP or Vista PC, you may come across one or two that refuse to run: this will be because they were designed for an earlier version of Windows. The solution is as follows:

With Vista, open the Control Panel in the Control Panel Home view and click Programs. Then click "Use an older program with this version of Windows". With XP, go to Start, All Programs, Accessories, Program Compatibility Wizard.

At the opening screen you'll have three options. Unless the program is on a CD/DVD, select the first option, "I want to choose from a list of programs". Click Next and Windows will show you a list of all the programs on the PC.

1 Select the program that won't run and click Next

Hot tip

Another way of applying compatibility settings is to right-click the program's executable (setup) file. Click Properties and then open the Compatibility tab. From here, you can choose the operating system that the program is known to work with.

2 Select an operating system with which the program is known to work, and click Next

Hot tip

If a program won't install at all, the method described on the left won't work. In this case, proceed as described in the margin tip above.

Windows will apply the compatibility settings and run the program. If it is now working OK, close the program and select "Yes, set this program to always use these compatibility settings". Click Next, and you're done.

Hot tip

Once a program has been successfully set up, it will use the compatibility settings every time it is run.

A Program won't Uninstall

This is a common problem, and is usually caused by uninstalling the program in question incorrectly. This mistake is often made in one of two ways:

- Right-clicking the program in All Programs and clicking Delete

- Right-clicking the program in the Program Files folder and clicking Delete

With the former, all you are doing is deleting a shortcut that leads to the program in the Program Files folder. With the latter, while you will delete the program's files, you will not delete any configuration changes the program has made to the system's settings. As a result, it is not completely uninstalled and thus may still be having an effect on the system.

The correct way to do it is as follows:

1 Go to Start, Control Panel

2 With Vista, click Programs and Features. With XP, click Add or Remove Programs

3 Select the program from the list, right-click it and click Uninstall

Hot tip

If you have already deleted a program's files from the Program Files folder, you will be unable to delete it correctly as described here. You will have to reinstall the program and then uninstall it in the correct manner.

A Device doesn't Work

You've connected a new device to your system but it doesn't work. There are two likely causes:

Missing Device Driver

You have not installed the device's driver software. This will be on the installation disc provided with the device. Place this in the CD/DVD drive and, when the installation screen appears, click the Install button.

The driver tells Windows that its associated device is there and asks for what it needs in the way of system resources. In most cases you will then have to reboot the PC to complete the installation.

When you are back in Windows, the device should then be operational. However, some devices – printers, scanners, and cable modems being typical examples – often require the driver to be installed *before* the device is connected to the PC.

If you've done the opposite, disconnect the device from the PC, uninstall the driver and then do it the correct way.

Bad or Incorrect Connections

Having made sure that the device has been installed correctly, if it still doesn't work then you have a connection issue.

If it's a peripheral device, such as a scanner or a printer, it will almost certainly be using a USB connection. Check that the connection is good and then try connecting the device to a different USB socket (it's not unheard-of for a socket to be faulty).

In the case of a plug-in device such as a sound or video card, check that the device is pushed home in its socket. If the device also has a cable connection to the system, as video cards have, check that this is connected correctly.

Hot tip

The best way of ensuring correct installation of a device is to read the installation instructions.
   While this may seem a statement of the obvious, it's amazing how many people neglect to do so.

...cont'd

The devices that are most commonly fitted incorrectly are speakers and video cards.

Speakers must be connected as shown here:

Most sound cards provide color-coded input and output jacks for easy identification.

Green – line out
Orange – line out
Black – line out
Blue – line in
Pink – microphone

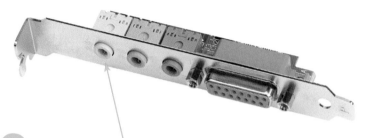

1 A two-speaker system connects to the green socket

2 With a multiple-speaker system, the green socket is used for the front speakers, the black socket for the rear speakers, and the orange sockets for the center and side speakers

If your system has both integrated video and a video card, check that you have connected the monitor to the correct system.

Incorrect connection of video cards usually occurs when the PC also has an built-in (integrated) motherboard video system. The mistake here is to connect the monitor to the wrong video system, i.e. to the integrated system rather than to the video card. This is a very easy mistake to make.

A New Hard Drive isn't Recognized

This can also be caused by incorrect connections but the usual cause is that the drive hasn't been partitioned and formatted. These two procedures prepare a new drive for use – partitioning creates a usable space on the drive and formatting creates a file system that is required by Windows.

If they are not done, while the PC will recognize the hard drive, the operating system will not: it will not appear in My Computer.

Although partitioning and formatting are relatively straightforward procedures, they are not within the scope of this book to describe and our purpose here is simply to make you aware of the potential problem. You will find many books and Internet sites that provide a full explanation.

Hard Drive Capacity is Incorrect

You've installed, partitioned and formatted a new hard drive. However, when you go to My Computer it is reported as being several GB smaller than it actually is. For example, a 250 GB drive will be reported as having a capacity of about 232 GB. So where has the missing capacity gone?

The answer is that there is actually no missing capacity. The discrepancy is the result of the hard drive manufacturers and the BIOS chip manufacturers using different measurement systems to calculate hard drive capacity.

The drive manufacturers define a GB as 1,000,000,000 bytes while the BIOS manufacturers define it as 1,073,741,824 bytes.

It's all in the mathematics and isn't a fault at all. The issue affects all hard drives and the bigger the drive, the more capacity appears to be missing.

How is a New User Account Set Up?

You want to add a user account but either don't know how or find the procedure confusing.

Hot tip

Standard or Limited accounts are intended for users who are not allowed to make system-wide changes. Restrictions include:

- Software and hardware cannot be installed.

- Account names and types cannot be changed.

- Only settings within the account can be changed. System-wide changes are not allowed.

1. Go to Start, Control Panel and click User Accounts

2. If you are using Windows XP, click "Create a new account". If you are using Windows Vista, click "Manage another account". In the next screen, click "Create a new account"

3. Give the account a suitable name and then select an account type – Administrator or Standard (Limited in Windows XP) – see top margin note

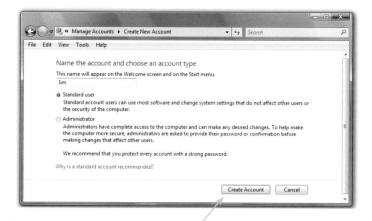

4. Then click Create Account. The next time you log on, you will have the option to use the new account

Hot tip

Guest accounts (available in Windows XP only) are similar to Limited accounts. These allow the computer to be used but no important settings to be changed. In addition, Guest users cannot access the Internet via a dial-up connection.

Regarding what type of account to create, the recommended option is Limited (XP) or Standard (Vista). This limits the user in terms of what can be done with the account and what changes can be made to the system.

However, if you are going to use the account yourself or you trust the user, select the Administrator option.

6 Disc Authoring

Creating your own CDs/DVDs is a popular activity. However, users do experience problems when writing discs. In this chapter we look at the more common ones.

Disc Write Fails

Many of the problems experienced in the early days of disc writing have been eliminated by the modern breed of CD/DVD writers and authoring programs. However, issues still remain, not a few of which are a result of users' lack of understanding of the subject rather than faults with the writing process itself.

For a disc to be written successfully, the flow of data from the source must be continuous and at a constant speed – otherwise the write will fail and usually the disc will be ruined. Anything that interrupts the data flow during the writing process can potentially cause errors. Therefore you need to track down and close anything on your PC that may be doing this.

The following are the usual causes of a failed write:

Windows AutoPlay Function

A few seconds into the write process, Windows will suddenly "see" the disc and try to read it. This will send an "interrupt" to the CPU, which can cause the write to fail.

Don't forget

The first thing to check if your disc writing fails is that the Windows AutoPlay function has been disabled.

For this reason many disc authoring programs will automatically disable AutoPlay. Some don't, however, so check it has been disabled on your system.

Background Activity

Disable all programs that operate invisibly in the background and can suddenly start to run, e.g. screensavers, antivirus software, disk management utilities, and Advanced Power Management.

Open Applications

Close all other programs that are running. These will be indicated on the Taskbar.

If the write still fails, check the following:

Write Method

Modern disc authoring programs use a write method known as Disc-at-once. Without going into the details, this is the most reliable method.

However, if you are using an older authoring program it may well be using a method known as Track-at-once. Here, data is written directly from the source to the disc. This is a fast method but also the most likely to result in a failed write as it does not check for errors.

If this is the case, look for an option called Disc Image. With this method the data is first saved to the hard drive as an image file, which allows potential problems to be identified.

Hot tip

There are several different methods of writing data to a disc. For reliability, Disc-at-once is currently the best.

Beware

The drawback with the Disc Image method is that the procedure will take twice as long. This is because the image file has to be created before it can be written to the disc.

1 Project being saved as an image file.

2 The image file is then written to the disc

...cont'd

Dual/Multi Booting

The likelihood of writing errors is increased if your authoring software is installed on a system that is part of a dual/multi boot setup. Try writing on a single-system setup.

Multiple Versions of Disc Authoring Software

Having two or more authoring programs installed is not good. These programs often use the same system files and resources and can thus prevent each other from working.

If this is the case, choose the one you want to use and uninstall the others.

Write Speed

Writing at too high a speed can cause errors. This applies particularly to systems with low CPU speed and memory capacity, which may struggle to cope with the flow of data as a result.

All authoring software has an option that will allow a slower write speed to be selected. An example is shown below:

Record Setup

Destination
F:\LITE-ON LTR-52327S

Number of Copies:
1

Write Speed
SmartBurn

☐ Copy to Hard Disk First
☑ Buffer Underrun Prevention

12x (1800KB/sec)
16x (2400KB/sec)
24x MAX
32x MAX

...tion will allow the recorder to automatically record at the optimal speed for the media being used. It is recommended that this option always be used to assure

roxio   OK   Cancel   Help   Details >>

Write speed options in Roxio's Easy CD Creator

Note that modern authoring programs select the optimum write speed automatically, although this can be overridden by the user.

Disc Read Fails

You've placed a disc to which you have written data in the CD/DVD drive but are unable to read its contents. There are two main causes of this:

UDF File Format

Also known as packet writing, UDF (Universal Disk Format) is a writing method that allows a CD or DVD to be used as you would a hard or floppy drive. Instead of having to use the authoring program to write the data, you simply drag it to the disc and it is written automatically.

All modern authoring programs offer the UDF option and it is a very easy way of writing discs. However, initially it can cause a lot of confusion because a disc written in the UDF format can only be read if the PC has packet writing software installed on it. Also, even if such software is installed, there is a possibility that it may not be compatible with the UDF software used to write the disc.

The way to check this out is as follows:

 Right-click the CD/DVD icon in My Computer and click Properties

If you see the following, the disc has been written in the UDF file format:

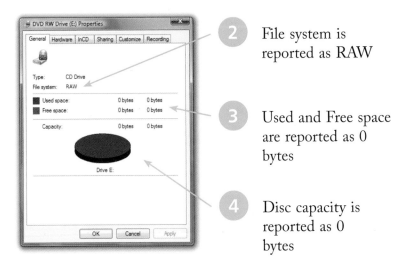

2   File system is reported as RAW

3   Used and Free space are reported as 0 bytes

4   Disc capacity is reported as 0 bytes

Beware

Before you can use the UDF method, the disc has to be formatted. This can reduce the disc's capacity by anything up to 20%.

Beware

UDF is not a reliable method of data storage. If you are planning on making a backup of important data, use the authoring program's "Data Disc" option.

...cont'd

If this is the case, you will need to install disc authoring software that offers the UDF option in order to read the disc. Also, as noted on the previous page, if you still can't read the disc, the UDF software that you have installed may be incompatible with the UDF software used to write the disc. In this situation, you may have to install that same program on your PC.

Note that Windows XP does not have native support for UDF whereas Windows Vista does. However, as explained above, Vista's version of UDF may not be compatible with that of other software manufacturers.

Disc Closing

A disc write procedure consists of three stages:

1) The lead-in area is created. This is an area at the start of each session that is left blank for the TOC (table of contents)

2) The data files are written

3) The lead-out area is created. This procedure writes out the table of contents in the lead-in area created at the beginning of the write and then closes the disc

If the final stage (lead-out) is missed out or nor completed then the disc will be unreadable as the TOC will be missing or incomplete. (Multi-session discs are an exception to this – see bottom margin note.)

A frequent cause of this problem is the user manually ejecting the disc before it has been properly closed. Alternatively, the computer may have frozen or crashed as the lead-out was being written.

Whatever the cause, this situation is irretrievable – if it's a write-once disc (CD-R or DVD-R), throw it away; if it's a rewritable disc (CD-RW or DVD-RW), you can reformat it and use it again.

Audio Discs won't Play

Home or car entertainment systems will only recognize music files recorded in the CDFS format. If music files are written using the authoring software's "Audio Disc" wizard, the files are automatically converted to this format.

However, if they are written with the UDF method, they will be in their original format – MP3, WAV, etc. Your PC's CD/DVD player will recognize them but a home or car player won't.

Check this out as follows:

1 In My Computer, right-click the disc and click Open. This will reveal the contents of the disc

Don't forget

If you intend creating a music disc to be played on a car or home CD/DVD player, you must write the music files using the CDFS file format.

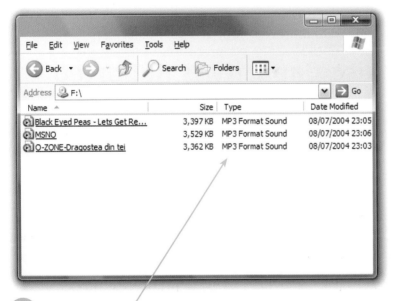

2 If the file type is anything other than CD Audio Track, then the files have been recorded in the wrong format, as shown in the example above

If you created the disc yourself you can simply redo it, this time using the authoring software's Audio Disc option. This will record the files in the correct format.

You Can't Add More Files to a Disc

You want to add some more files to a music disc you created earlier, as you can when writing data. However, the authoring program won't let you – it just says "The disc inserted is not blank".

This is not actually a fault – it's done by design. The reason is that you can only add files to a multi-session (open) disc, which is what modern authoring software will create by default when you write data.

However, many home and car CD players can't read multi-session discs so most authoring software will create a single-session (closed) disc, which they can read, when you burn music files. Because the disc has been closed, however, you cannot add more files to it at a later date.

Disc Capacity is Reported Incorrectly

Windows reports your 700 MB CD as having approximately 550 MB of free space.

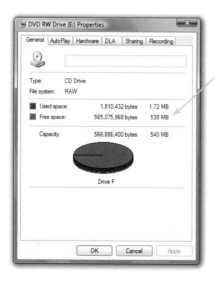

Free space is reported as being 538 MB

This isn't a fault but rather is due to the disc having being formatted by UDF software. Typically, the formatting procedure uses some 150 MB of a CD's capacity. A DVD will lose even more.

Copied Software Discs won't Play

Software piracy is a serious problem for the manufacturers, so not surprisingly they have come up with methods designed to minimize the practice. These take various forms, two of the most common being copy-protection and product activation.

As a typical example of this, you've borrowed a program from a friend or downloaded it from the Internet, copied it to a disc and then tried to install it. However, it won't work – you get a "Please Insert Disk" or similar message, as shown above.

This is copy-protection at work, and basically it ensures that the program can only be installed from the original (genuine) disc. The method is commonly used by games manufacturers.

Trying to circumvent copy-protection, product activation and similar anti-piracy measures is illegal. Do not be tempted to use the tools that are made available on some websites on the Internet for this purpose.

File Attributes are Locked

You've tried to change the attributes of a file on a disc, perhaps to compress or hide it. You get an error message, though, saying "Access is Denied". This will happen if the disc in question is a write-once disc as you can only write to these once. The only solution in this case is to copy the file to the hard drive, change the attributes and then write it to a new disc. However, you can change file attributes on a rewritable disc.

Third-Party Software

While most people will be quite content with the functional but somewhat limited disc authoring utility provided with Windows, some will prefer the additional features and options offered by programs such as Roxio's Easy CD Creator.

However, some third-party authoring software does not integrate well with Windows and can cause the following problems:

- A "Drive is not Accessible" error message appears
- The CD/DVD drive is missing from My Computer
- The Recording tab is missing from the drive's Properties
- The drive is not recognized as a recordable device

Hot tip

There are other causes for the errors detailed on this page. If you are experiencing any of these and you don't have third-party authoring programs installed, have a look on the Microsoft website. There are several articles offering causes and solutions. You can also find answers in the many Internet forums available on the subject of disc writing.

74

If you experience any of these problems, uninstall all third-party authoring software. If you can identify a particular program as causing problems but still want to use it, go to the manufacturer's website for any available patches.

Roxio's Easy CD Creator version 5.01 and DirectCD 3.01d or earlier are known to cause the problems detailed above. If you wish to use these particular applications, you should upgrade to the latest versions.

While on the subject of upgrading, it is also a good idea to upgrade the firmware of your CD/DVD drive, particularly if it is an older model. Firmware upgrades are available for download from the relevant manufacturers' websites.

7 Video and Sound

The elements of sound and video probably give rise to more problems with computers than any others. This chapter gives you the lowdown on these issues.

No Display (Monitor is Blank)

There are three situations in which you may encounter a display that is completely blank:

- When you boot the computer
- When Windows begins to load
- When Windows is running

The first scenario (a blank monitor when the PC boots) indicates a hardware problem. Refer to Chapter Two for details on how to troubleshoot this.

If the display goes blank at the point where Windows begins to load, the most likely causes are:

- The video driver is corrupt
- The video BIOS settings are incorrect

Repair the video driver as follows:

1. Reboot the PC into Safe Mode as described on page 35

2. When you are back in Windows, go to Start, All Programs, Accessories, System Tools, System Restore

3. Run System Restore and select a restore point that was made on a day when the PC was working OK

When the restore procedure is complete, the problem should be resolved.

However, if it is not or you are unable to use System Restore for some reason (it might be disabled for example), then you will have to reinstall the video driver. Do this as follows:

1. Reboot the PC in Safe Mode again and, when you are back in Windows, go to the Device Manager – see margin note

Hot tip

To access the Device Manager in Windows Vista, go to Start, Control Panel, Device Manager.

If you are using Windows XP, go to Start, Control Panel, System, Hardware, Device Manager.

2 Right-click your video driver (in the "Display adapter" category) and click Uninstall

Hot tip

If your system is using a video system integrated into the motherboard, the video driver will be on the disk supplied with the motherboard. If you have a separate video card, the driver will be on the disk supplied with the card.

3 Place the video driver CD (see margin note) in the CD/DVD drive and follow the prompts at the installation screen to install the driver

4 When the installation is complete, reboot the PC

The display should now be restored. However, if the problem occurred after you installed a new video card or altered settings in the BIOS, you need to do the following:

1 Reboot the PC and enter the BIOS setup program as described on page 37

2 Locate the key that loads the BIOS fail-safe defaults

77

...cont'd

Hot tip

Should you carry out this procedure, we recommend you first go through the BIOS and make a written note of all the settings. This will be time-consuming but will enable you subsequently to restore the settings to the way they were.

3 Press the key specified (often it is the F6 key), save the changes and exit the BIOS

4 Reboot the computer and the display should now be restored

This procedure loads a conservative set of BIOS settings that is pretty much guaranteed to work with any setup.

Be aware that doing this will also undo any performance-enhancing changes that might previously have been made to the BIOS. These will have been done by the computer's manufacturer and possibly by yourself. When the system is up and running again you should go back to the BIOS and redo these changes.

Don't let this put you off, however. Simply make a written note of the existing settings before you do it. Alternatively, there are any number of websites offering full instructions on how to set up a BIOS optimally.

If the display has been working OK and then suddenly goes blank after a period of inactivity, check the following:

Advanced Power Management

Hot tip

In Windows Vista, APM is known as a Power Plan.

Advanced Power Management (APM) is a Windows application that allows the user to set a time after which specific parts of the PC are placed in standby mode or switched off. In the case of a monitor, this has the effect of blanking the screen.

In theory a slight movement of the mouse, or pressing a key, will bring the monitor back to life – but it doesn't always work like that. Sometimes it can take a considerable amount of mouse-clicking and key-bashing to get the monitor display back again.

Make sure this isn't the cause of the problem before going any further. If necessary, reboot the PC to be sure.

If APM is the cause of the problem you can disable it, or change its settings, to prevent a recurrence. Alternatively, you can specify a longer period before APM kicks in.

1. If you are running Windows Vista go to Start, Control Panel, Power Options. At the first screen, select an appropriate power plan

Advanced Power Management (APM) is a Windows feature that is designed for the users of laptop computers. It enables these users to configure power saving settings that enable the laptop's battery power to be conserved as much as possible.

For example, the computer can be configured to switch itself to Standby mode after a specified period. Individual components such as the hard drive and the monitor can also be configured in the same way.

This last setting can be the cause of a seemingly dead monitor.

2. At the next screen, select the most suitable power settings. To disable APM, choose the Never option

Windows XP users can access their APM settings by right-clicking the Desktop and selecting Properties, Screensavers, Settings.

Display Flickers

Staring for hours at a display that is flickering very slightly, even if the flicker is almost imperceptible, is guaranteed to scramble your brains eventually. This is an old problem that can occur with a cathode ray tube (CRT) monitor and is caused by the display's refresh rate being set too low.

If you are running Windows Vista, check it out as follows:

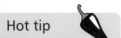
1 Right-click the Desktop and click Personalize, Display Settings, Advanced Settings, Monitor tab

Generic PnP Monitor and NVIDIA GeForce 6200   Properties

Adapter | Monitor | Troubleshoot | Color Management | GeForce 6200

Monitor Type

Generic PnP Monitor

Properties

Monitor Settings

Screen refresh rate:

75 Hertz

56 Hertz
60 Hertz
72 Hertz
75 Hertz

monitor cannot display correctly. This may lead to an unusable display and/or damaged hardware.

OK   Cancel   Apply

2 Choose the highest available refresh rate. Then click OK

The screen will now go blank for a few seconds before a dialog box appears, asking if you want to keep the new setting. Click Yes to accept the new refresh rate.

If you are using Windows XP, access the refresh rate dialog box by right-clicking the Desktop and clicking Properties, the Settings tab, Advanced and, finally, the Monitor tab.

Display is Scrambled

The screen is a unintelligible mass of lines. This problem can occur for two reasons:

- The refresh rate is set too high

- The screen resolution is set too high

The procedure for resolving both of the above is as follows:

1   Restart the PC and go to Startup Options by tapping the F8 key as the computer boots

2   Use the arrow keys to select Enable VGA Mode. Press Enter

Windows will now load a generic video driver, which will clear the scrambled display and thus allow you to find out what's causing the problem.

The first thing to try is setting a lower refresh rate. Set the rate as described on page 80. Then reboot the PC normally and, if the problem is still present, do the following:

1   Repeat steps one and two above

2   Windows Vista users should right-click the Desktop and click Personalize, Display Settings. XP users should right-click the Desktop and click Properties and the Settings tab

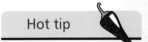

Hot tip

Video Graphics Array (VGA) is a basic video display system for PCs and provides a screen resolution of 640 x 480 with 16 colors.

All computers are capable of using this system, and because of this it is useful when troubleshooting video problems.

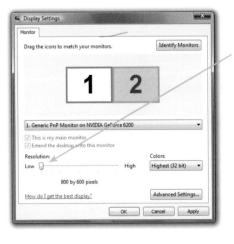

3   Reduce the resolution by dragging the slider back

4   Reboot, and the problem should be resolved

Display is Very Slow

When a graphic (image) is loaded, such as the Windows startup screen, it does not appear instantly. Instead, you can literally see it being drawn on the screen by the video system. This is quite a common problem and is the result of the video driver having been uninstalled (intentionally or otherwise) or having become corrupted. In this situation Windows takes over and installs a basic VGA video driver, which will work with all setups.

However, while it will provide a picture, it will be slow. Check this out as follows:

Hot tip

Another way of checking your video driver is by looking in the Device Manager. Details of the driver currently installed will be found under "Display adapter".

1 XP users should right-click the Desktop and click Properties, Settings, Advanced, Adapter.
Vista users should right-click the Desktop and click Personalize, Display Settings, Adapter

82

Generic PnP Monitor and NVIDIA GeForce 6200 Properties

| Adapter | Monitor | Troubleshoot | Color Management | GeForce 6200 |

Adapter Type

Properties

Adapter Information

Chip Type: <unavailable>
DAC Type: <unavailable>
Memory Size: <unavailable>
Adapter String: <unavailable>
Bios Information: <unavailable>

List All Modes...

OK   Cancel   Apply

2 If there is nothing listed under Adapter Type then your video driver has been uninstalled or is corrupt

3 Place the video driver CD in the CD/DVD drive. Then click the Properties button in the Adapter dialog box, click the Driver tab and then click Update Driver. This opens the Add Hardware wizard. Click Next and follow the prompts to reinstall the driver

No Sound

Your computer is not producing any sound. The first thing to establish is whether the problem applies to the whole system or just to parts of it.

First, try playing a music disc in the CD/DVD drive. If that doesn't work try playing a WAV file as described below.

1 Go to Start, Control Panel, Sound (or Sounds and Audio Devices if you are running Windows XP)

2 Select a sound file

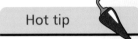
If the problem occurs after upgrading your system to Windows XP or Vista, there is a good possibility that your sound system is not compatible with these operating systems. You may need to download an updated driver from the manufacturer's website to get it working.

83

Sound

| Playback | Recording | Sounds |

A sound theme is a set of sounds applied to events in Windows and programs. You can select an existing scheme or save one you have modified.

Sound Scheme:

Windows Default (modified) ▼   [Save As...]   [Delete]

To change sounds, click a program event in the following list and then select a sound to apply. You can save the changes as a new sound scheme.

Program

- Windows
  - Asterisk
  - Close program
  - Critical Battery Alarm
  - Critical Stop
  - Default Beep

☑ Play Windows Startup sound

Sounds:

Windows Battery Critical.wav ▼   [▶ Test]   [Browse...]

[OK]   [Cancel]   [Apply]

3 Click Test

If either of these tests produces sound then the problem is not too serious as they indicate that the sound system, speakers and speaker connections are all OK. The problem will be specific to a particular application. Reinstalling the application in question will usually fix the problem.

If, however, you can't get any sound at all then you need to investigate further.

Checking the Sound System

The first thing to check is your sound system.

1 Go to Start, Control Panel, Sound (or Sound and Audio Devices if you are running Windows XP)

2 If there is nothing listed on the Playback and Recording tabs then the sound system driver is missing or corrupt

3 Place the sound driver CD in the CD/DVD drive and follow the prompts to reinstall the sound driver

4 When the installation is complete, reboot the PC and your sound will now be restored

Checking the Speakers

If the sound driver checks out OK then the problem will be with the speakers or the sound volume controls.

Volume Controls

First, check the Windows volume control. If you see a speaker icon in the Notification area, click it to open the volume control dialog box. If necessary, adjust the relevant sliders to increase the volume. Also, check that Mute hasn't been selected.

If you don't see an icon in the Notification area then go to Start, Control Panel, Sound (or Sound and Audio Devices if you are running Windows XP). Click the Volume tab and then adjust the sliders as necessary. (Note that there is also an option here that allows you to place the speaker icon in the Notification area.)

Second, check the volume control on the speakers themselves (if they have one – some do, some don't).

Speakers

First, if your speakers are of the powered type, check that they are receiving power.

Second, check that the speakers are connected to the system correctly as described on page 62. If your system has a sound card, be sure to check that the speakers are connected to this rather than to the integrated motherboard sound system.

If everything checks out OK then the speakers themselves are faulty. The easiest way to check this possibility is to connect them to a different sound system, such as your Hi-Fi system.

However, this is very unlikely. The usual cause of lack of sound is the sound driver.

Hot tip

A common mistake when connecting speakers to a PC is to connect them to the wrong sound system, i.e. integrated audio instead of a sound card, or vice versa.

Distorted Sound

This problem can be caused by an excessively high volume level or a mismatch between speaker volume level and sound device volume level. Adjust it as follows:

1. Turn the volume control on your speakers to its middle position

2. Open the Windows volume control as described on the previous page. Click the Volume tab and then Advanced. Adjust the volume slider to a comfortable level

Hot tip

If your sound hisses and crackles, the cause will be electrical interference from nearby power sources.

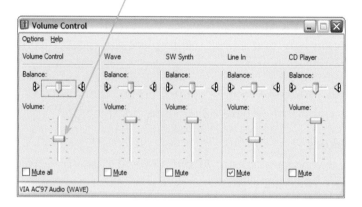

Jerky or Intermittent Sound

A common cause of this is a damaged or incompatible sound driver; reinstall it. If the problem is still there, go to the manufacturer's website and download the latest driver.

This problem can also be caused by a system that is struggling to cope with the demands made on it, and on the memory in particular. Close any other applications that may be running to ease the load on the PC. If this doesn't work, try rebooting the PC to return it to a stable condition.

Yet another possibility is a corrupt sound codec – see page 88. In this case you will have to identify the codec in question and then download and install a good version from the Internet.

8 Multimedia

Multimedia is a very important aspect of computing these days.

Movies won't Play or have No Sound

Missing Codecs

You've clicked a video file but, instead of playing it, your media player just plays a visualization as shown below. Alternatively, depending on the player, you may get an error message stating that a codec is missing.

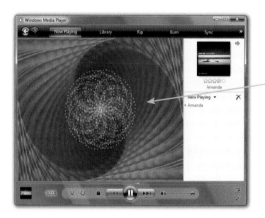

Visualizations are very pretty but you'd rather see your movie

Hot tip

Codecs are used for both video and sound, so you may have a situation in which your movie plays but without any sound.

The solution is the same – identify the missing codec and download it from the Internet.

When this happens it means that the media player hasn't been able to find the correct codec. Codecs are small software programs that are used to compress a video or sound file when it is created in order to reduce the file size. When the file is played it is decompressed and, to do that, the codec that compressed it must be on the computer.

The most-used type of video codec is AVI (Audio-Video Interleaved) of which there are many versions. The two most common are called DIVX and XVID. If you get the above problem, you should download and install both of these codecs as it's very likely that the file has been compressed with one or the other. You can find them at www.divxmovies.com.

However, there are many different types of codec and so it may be that your movie or sound file still won't play. In this situation, you need to know the codec used by the file. Go to www.headbands.com/gspot and download a program called Gspot. Open the video file in Gspot and you will be able to see the codec that it uses. Then do an Internet search for this.

Movie Playback is Poor

Hardware Issues

Your movies are jerky or flicker, or you see lines on the screen.

The above issues are often a result of an underpowered system and will be most noticeable when playing movies from a DVD. Check that your CPU and memory are up to scratch. If they are not, you will have to upgrade them.

Check that DirectX is correctly installed as described on page 90. Also, upgrade it to the latest version. The same applies to your video driver – a lot of problems are caused by outdated or incompatible video drivers.

If the video is a Windows Media Video (WMV) file, turn on DirectX video acceleration as decribed below:

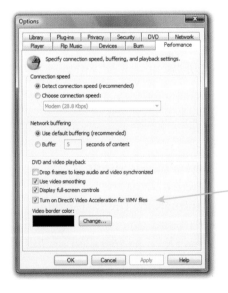

Hot tip

Windows Media Player (WMP) is tightly integrated with several operating system components, DirectX in particular.

Therefore any problems with DirectX can have serious knock-on effects with Windows Media Player.

1 From the Tools menu in Windows Media Player select Options and then click the Performance tab

2 Check the "Turn on DirectX Video Acceleration ..." checkbox

Beware

Many codec packs are untested compilations of various codecs and filters commonly used on the Internet. These can cause problems.

Codec Problems

If playback is still poor then you probably have a problem with the codecs installed on your system.

This particular issue is often caused by the various codec packs available on the Internet. Incompatibilities are known to exist with some of the components in these packs, which can cause playback problems. If you have any of these packs on your system, uninstall them.

Games don't Play Properly

There are probably not too many senior citizens who play PC games, but for those who do the following may be useful.

Hardware Requirements

Of all the applications that can be run on a PC, games can be the most demanding in terms of hardware requirements. If your system is not up to scratch, you will have problems. Check the game's recommended system requirements, which will be listed on the box and in the documentation. Then see if your system is up to the required specifications. If not, you may have to upgrade it. Before you do, though, try a few simple steps that can sometimes free up enough resources to make the difference:

- Switch off and then restart the PC. This will clear the memory – see top margin note

- Make sure no other applications are running

- Lower your screen resolution as described on page 81

- Set up Windows for best performance (as opposed to best appearance) as described on page 53

DirectX

DirectX is a technology developed by Microsoft that facilitates the display of multimedia elements, such as full color graphics, video, and 3D animation. The majority of modern PC games are written around this technology and require a specific version of DirectX to be installed on the computer. Check it out as follows:

1. Go to Start, Run. In the Run box, type Dxdiag and click OK. When the DirectX diagnostic utility opens, click the System tab. At the bottom of the dialog box, you'll see which version of DirectX you have

2. If your version of DirectX needs to be updated, you will find the latest version on the Microsoft website available as a free download. (It is worth having the latest version whether you play games or not)

Hot tip

Closing an application doesn't necessarily mean it will release the memory it was using. Sometimes programs will leave fragments of themselves behind.

The only way to completely clear the memory is to switch off the PC as it will retain data as long as it is powered up.

Hot tip

DirectX enables programmers to write programs without knowing exactly what hardware will be installed on users' PCs.

Internet Streaming Problems

Streaming is watching, or listening to, a media file on the Internet in real time. The file is streamed from a server and received and stored in a temporary buffer on your computer. It is not saved on your hard drive.

Media File Doesn't Play

You click on an Internet media file but your media player won't play it. The usual cause of this is that your browser is not configured to open the file.

If you are using Internet Explorer, the file will open in Windows Media Player (WMP). However, if you are using a different browser, such as Mozilla Firefox or Opera, you will have to configure WMP (or your media player of choice) as the default media player. You will find the necessary settings in the browser's Options menu.

The problem could also be those pesky codecs again (see pages 88–89). If your media player can't find the necessary codec on your system, it can't play the file.

Another, less likely, possibility is that the file is corrupt.

Playback is Intermittent

This is a common problem, which is almost always due to a slow Internet connection. This results in the flow of data to the computer being too slow, which in turn prevents the buffer from being replenished quickly enough.

When the buffer on the PC is empty, media playback stops. The thing to do here is to increase the size of the buffer so that the effect of network congestion is less.

Assuming WMP is your media player, go to Options on its Tools menu and click the Performance tab. Deselect the default buffer setting of five seconds, and in the box enter a higher figure – ten seconds to begin with.

See how you go with that. If necessary, keep raising the setting until the problem is resolved.

Hot tip

Hopefully it goes without saying that for successful Internet streaming you will need a fast broadband connection.

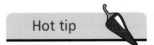

Hot tip

When you click a media streaming file, the buffer on the PC is loaded before the file starts to play. So the larger you make the buffer, the longer it will be before the file is ready to play.

Photo Editing Problems

Hot tip

If you have an image that cannot be replaced, make a copy and use that for editing. If you mess it up, you've still got the original.

Hot tip

The JPEG format, which is commonly used by digital cameras, is a lossy format.

Hot tip

The imaging program provided by Windows is very limited in terms of editing facilities. If you're serious about your photos, we suggest you acquire Corel Paintshop Pro, or a program with similar capabilities.

Calibrate the Monitor

The first thing you must do is calibrate your monitor. If it is incorrectly set up then no matter how carefully you edit your images, when you print them or view them on a different monitor they will look different. Calibration software may be provided with your monitor. If not, download a suitable application from the Internet.

Covert the Image to a Lossless Format

Image formats are either lossy or lossless. Every time a lossy image is edited, some loss of image data occurs. Thus, the more times it is edited, the worse the end result. Lossless images, on the other hand, can be edited any number of times with no loss of quality.

So before you edit any image of a lossy type, e.g. JPEG, convert it to either a TIFF or a PNG format, both of which are lossless. Having edited the image, convert it back to the original file type. This ensures that the original image quality is retained.

Brightness and Contrast Adjustments

All image editors provide brightness and contrast controls, and often a one-click setting that does the job automatically. While these can work well, sometimes the result is less than optimal.

A better, and more reliable, way is to use the image editor's Histogram control (shown below). This gives a graphical representation of the image, showing its color distribution in terms of brightness and darkness. The left of the graph represents black and the right represents white. Consider the badly under-exposed picture shown below:

The histogram of the image on page 92 shows that its data is over to the left of the graph, i.e. its dark tones are overemphasized (if an image's exposure is correct, the data will be centered in the graph).

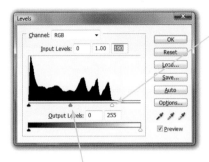

1 Drag the white pointer to where the data begins. This sets the image's brightness to the correct level

2 Now adjust the gray pointer in the middle to set the image's contrast

Color Correction

The next adjustment to make is to the image's colors. This is done with the Hue/Saturation control (shown below). A common mistake is to adjust all the colors simultaneously until the picture "looks about right". However, this often results in one color being correct and the others being incorrect.

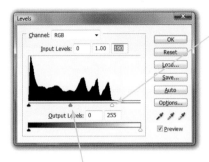

The right way to do it is to edit each color individually by selecting it from the Edit menu. Adjustments will thus affect that color only.

An example is shown on the next page.

...cont'd

Hot tip

Another way to adjust the color of a specific area of an image is to select the area with a selection tool such as the Marquee or Lasso tool. Any changes you make will affect the selected area only.

In this image, the grass and trees have a yellowish tint that gives a slightly washed-out or faded look

Adjusting only green gives the grass and trees a more natural color, while the other colors remain unchanged

Sharpening

The first rule of image sharpening is that this process should be the last edit to be made. The second rule is to ignore the Sharpen and Sharpen More tools, as they provide little user control and usually result in the image being sharpened incorrectly.

Hot tip

Sharpening tools should be used with restraint. Overuse of them will ruin your images.

The tool you should use is the Unsharp Mask. When using this, you need to zoom in closely so that you can work with precision.

Many imaging programs provide a zoom-in preview window for this purpose. If yours doesn't, use the program's zoom control to get in close.

The rule of thumb is to look for halos along sharp edges. When you see these, reduce the Threshold setting until the halos disappear. Then you should be about right.

9 The Internet

This chapter looks at problems experienced when using the Internet. These range from inability to access specific sites, to broken and slow connections.

You are Unable to Connect

There are two likely reasons for this:

- Your Internet Service Provider (ISP) is down

- Your modem is faulty, or its connections are

Internet Service Provider
Examine the front panel LEDs on your broadband modem and look for the one that indicates whether or not the modem is receiving data.

If it's lit, this tells you that the ISP's servers are OK, and that the incoming connection to the modem is as well. However, if it isn't, either the ISP's servers are down (most likely) or you have a connection problem between the cable input to the house and the modem (less likely).

The simplest way to establish which is the cause of the problem is to rule out the ISP first by telephoning and asking whether there is a problem.

Modem
First, check the connection between the modem and the PC. Do this by observing the appropriate LED on the modem. If this is out, check the cable connections at both ends.

Second, check that the modem is correctly installed. Open the Device Manager and, under the "Network adapters" category, make sure your modem is listed. If it isn't, the modem driver is corrupt. Reinstall it from the installation disc.

Third, occasionally broadband modems will lose contact with the ISP. This can be due to a problem at the ISP's end or to a power outage at the users end; there are other causes as well. Whichever it is, the user loses his or her connection.

The solution to this problem is to "power cycle" the modem. Do this by switching the PC off, disconnecting the modem and then reconnecting it before switching the PC back on. Without going into the reasons, this will re-establish your connection.

Hot tip

Most ISPs provide a recorded telephone message that gives details of any areas in which they are experiencing technical problems. A quick phone call can save you a lot of time hunting about for non-existent faults.

Hot tip

Many ISPs provide a diagnostic utility on their installation disc. This can be used to resolve modem configuration issues.

Your Connection is Slow

Websites take longer than usual to load; file download speeds are abnormally slow. This problem can be due to Internet conditions, your ISP or the computer.

The Internet

If the Internet is the source of the problem, the cause will be network congestion. However, congestion is rarely, if ever, endemic to the entire Internet network and will almost always be restricted to an individual ISP or website. Check a few familiar sites and if they all load slowly you can eliminate network congestion as the problem.

Internet Service Provider (ISP)

Many, if not most, low-cost broadband packages deliver a slower connection speed than promised. The reason this is so is that ISPs can only make these packages pay by giving each user a small amount of bandwidth – see margin note. If you have recently subscribed to one of these packages, this is likely to be the source of the problem – either accept it or upgrade to a more expensive, and so probably better, package.

However, if your connection is normally good but has suddenly become less so, it could be a temporary technical issue at the ISP's end. Contact them to see if this is the case.

Your Computer

There are three issues at the user's end that can reduce the speed of a broadband connection.

The first is a PC that simply doesn't have the hardware resources required to handle the demands made of it by broadband. If your connection has always been slower than it should be, this is the most likely explanation. The solution here is to increase the amount of memory in your system and, if that doesn't help, install a faster CPU.

As a guide, broadband requires a memory capacity of 125 MB at the minimum (we recommend 250 MB). CPU speed is less important, but even so you should have one that runs at no less than 233 MHz (500 MHz or higher is recommended).

Hot tip

All broadband providers share the available bandwidth between users. The amount an individual user gets is known as the contention ratio.

For example, if the service is contended at 20:1, it means that you share the bandwidth with up to 19 other users.

The cheaper your package, the higher the contention ratio (and thus the slower the connection) is likely to be.

Hot tip

Hardware requirements are only likely to be an issue with older computers.

...cont'd

However, if your connection speed has dropped off abruptly, or even gradually, the problem will lie elsewhere. The most likely cause is that your computer has become infected with malware – see page 144.

Without going into the reasons, these pernicious programs can slow your Internet connection (and, indeed, your entire computer) to an alarming degree.

The most obvious indications that you have malware, apart from the slowing down of your connection or your PC, are the sudden appearance of toolbars in your browser, automatic redirection of your browser to advertising sites, sites added to your Favorites list, and a profusion of pop-up windows. Many malware programs, though, are more subtle and present no obvious signs of their presence.

The solution is to detect and uninstall them, and to this end you will need a malware removal program. Two of the best known are Ad-aware (www.lavasoft.com), shown below, and Spybot Search & Destroy (www.safer-networking.org). These are both available as free downloads and will rid your PC of unwelcome malware.

Hot tip

Windows Vista provides users with a built-in anti-malware utility called Windows Defender. This can be accessed via the Control Panel.

98

Don't forget

Poor cable connections can be the cause of slow connection speeds.

The final thing to check is that your broadband connections are sound. Start with the connection to the house, then the cable input to the modem, and finally the connection to the computer from the modem.

Websites or Pages are Inaccessible

There are a number of reasons why you may not be able to access a certain website or web page. The following are the most common.

Site Congestion

Popular sites, such as the Microsoft site for example, can at times become extremely congested with thousands of users all trying to access them simultaneously. If it can't load the site, your browser will eventually give up and display a "Page cannot be displayed" error message. The only thing you can do in this situation is to try again later.

Cookies

If you are unable to access a specific page within a website, the usual reason is that your browser is configured not to accept cookies – see top margin note. Be aware that some sites will refuse access to a page if they are unable to place their cookie on a user's PC – a typical example of this is when they have password-protected pages.

Check this out as follows:

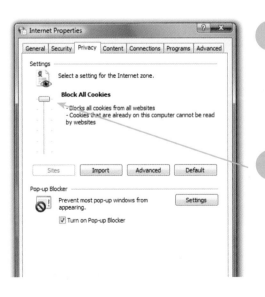

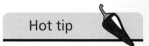

Hot tip

Cookies are small text files that websites download to users' PCs. They are used to track user activity on a website and to store user information and preferences.

This allows sites to customize pages when a user revisits the site.

Hot tip

While the vast majority of cookies are harmless, some can be used to access information on PCs. For this reason, many users disable cookies.

1 Open Internet Options in the Control Panel and click the Privacy tab

2 Make sure the slider is not set to Block All Cookies. If it is, then drag it down a level

...cont'd

On a related note, many web pages contain embedded controls or programs. When you click the link, the program or control should run. However, it will only do so if you have the program installed on your PC.

Typical examples of this are Adobe Flash Player, which is used by many sites to display video; and Java, a common use of which is for the calendars found on travel booking sites. If you don't have the program in question installed, you will usually get a message saying which one is required, and a link to a website from which you can download it.

Firewalls

A firewall is a program that prevents people accessing the computers of other users via the Internet – an activity commonly known as hacking.

Unfortunately, firewalls can sometimes do the opposite, i.e. prevent a user from accessing websites. So, if you are having access problems and have a firewall installed, try disabling it.

Assuming you are using the firewall provided by Windows, do this as follows:

Hot tip

If you have an "always on" broadband connection, you should have a firewall enabled. So if you disable it to see whether it is interfering with your Internet access, don't forget to re-enable it.

1   If you are running Windows XP, go to Start, Control Panel, Network Connections. Right-click your connection and click Properties and then the Advanced tab. Under Internet Connection Firewall, uncheck the "Protect my computer" checkbox

2   If you are running Windows Vista, go to Start, Control Panel, Windows Firewall. Click Change Settings and then check the Off checkbox

If this resolves the issue then you may need to reconfigure the firewall's settings to prevent a recurrence. We don't have space to describe this procedure here but you will find many websites that provide full instructions.

Script Debug Error Messages

A common problem that can occur when browsing the Internet with Internet Explorer is the sudden appearance of Script Debug error messages.

They usually say something like "Script error at line 01. Do you wish to debug?" These messages can be persistent, and thus extremely irritating.

Get rid of them as follows:

1 Go to Start, Control Panel, Internet Options

2 Click the Advanced tab

3 Scroll down to Disable Script Debugging and check the box

Hot tip

There are three causes of script debug error messages:
First, the web page author has made a programming error. Second, you may be running a pop-up blocker that closes pop-up windows so fast that the script on the web page fails. Third, you might have malware installed on your computer that activates the script error messages.

When Internet Explorer detects an error on a page it launches a script debugger to diagnose the problem.

Whenever one of the messages appears, always choose No from the options it gives.

101

Internet Properties

General | Security | Privacy | Content | Connections | Programs | **Advanced**

Settings

- Accessibility
  - ☐ Always expand ALT text for images
  - ☐ Move system caret with focus/selection changes
  - ☐ Reset text size to medium for new windows and tabs
  - ☑ Reset text size to medium while zooming*
  - ☑ Reset Zoom level to 100% for new windows and tabs
- Browsing
  - ☐ Close unused folders in History and Favorites*
  - ☑ Disable script debugging (Internet Explorer)
  - ☐ Disable script debugging (Other)
  - ☐ Display a notification about every script error
  - ☑ Enable FTP folder view (outside of Internet Explorer)
  - ☑ Enable page transitions
  - ☐ Enable personalized favorites menu

*Takes effect after you restart Internet Explorer

[Restore advanced settings]

Reset Internet Explorer settings

Deletes all temporary files, disables browser add-ons, and resets all the changed settings.

[Reset...]

You should only use this if your browser is in an unusable state.

4 Uncheck the "Display a notification about every script error" checkbox

Get Rid of Browser Pop-Up Windows

Hot tip

Pop-ups can be useful so most pop-up blockers allow the user to accept pop-ups from specified sites and block them from others.

Hot tip

Not all pop-up blockers are created equal. Some block all pop-ups while others are more "intelligent" and allow legitimate content to be displayed.

Hot tip

Most pop-up blockers provide a manual override key (usually the CTRL key). Hold the key down when you click the link and any pop-ups associated with the link will be allowed.

If used for the right purpose, such as displaying useful information, pop-up windows are an acceptable part of browsing the Internet. Unfortunately, however, they are all too often used to display irritating advertisements and other such stuff.

The solution to this problem is to use a pop-up blocker. These programs automatically prevent a website opening pop-up windows in your browser.

Users of Windows Vista have a built-in pop-up blocker. However, if you are using Windows XP or an earlier Windows version, you will either have to install Internet Explorer 7 (a free download from www.microsoft.com), or install a third-party pop-up blocker.

A quick search of the Internet will reveal dozens of these, some good, some not so good.

One that we recommend comes with the Google Toolbar (a useful browser add-on in itself). Download this from http://toolbar.google.com.

The Google pop-up blocker

Another option is to download and install a third-party browser. For example, the Firefox browser (available free from www.mozilla.com) comes with a built-in pop-up blocker. Furthermore, Firefox is generally considered to be a superior browser to Internet Explorer 7.

Where Did that Downloaded File Go?

You've downloaded a file from the Internet but you can't find it on your PC.

If you are running any version of Internet Explorer, by default the downloaded file will be placed on the Desktop. So this is the first place to look.

However, you may have selected a different location in the "Save As" dialog box and then forgotten it. Alternatively, you may have selected a different location inadvertently. You may also be using a third-party browser such as Opera or Firefox, both of which have a different default download location.

In any of these scenarios, you will have no idea where the file is. You have two options:

Hot tip

Third-party browsers usually have a different default download folder from that of Internet Explorer. You will be able to see which it is (and also change it) from Options on the Tools menu.

The first is to return to the web page (or any page that offers a file for download) containing the file and click the download link.

The "Save As" dialog box will open, and in the address box you will see the Save location. Make a note of it, cancel the download and then go the specified location on your PC. This is where the downloaded file will be.

The second option is to use the Windows Search utility (see page 159) to locate the file. If you can remember the name of the file, use that as the search parameter. Otherwise, do a search by date.

Hot tip

All browsers will save a download in the location used for the previous download by default.

Quick Internet Searching

Search engines certainly speed up the process of finding something specific on the Internet. However, simply typing in a relevant word and clicking Go is not the most efficient way to use them.

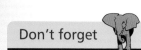
For example: type the word "tiger" in Google and you will get millions of pages to look through. These will range from the Tiger Lily restaurant in Shanghai and Tiger Woods the golfer to, not surprisingly, pages about tigers. Finding something specific can take a long time.

So, to help users narrow their searches, all the major search engines offer an Advanced Search. This will offer various options, such as language-specific searches, searches restricted to pages updated within a specific time-frame, etc.

However, before you try these, the following simple search aids may be all you need.

Phrase Searches

By enclosing your keywords in quotation marks, you will do a phrase search. This will return pages with all the keywords in the order entered. For example, "atlanta falcons" will return pages mainly concerning the Atlanta NFL team. Most pages regarding Atlanta (the city) or falcons (the birds) will be excluded.

The - Operator

The - operator allows you to exclude words from a search. For example, if you are looking for windows (glass ones), type: windows -microsoft -vista -xp -me -98 -2000 -nt

This will eliminate millions of pages devoted to the various Windows operating systems.

The + Operator

Most search engines exclude common words such as "and" and "to", and certain single digits and letters. If you want to make sure a common word is included in the search, type + before it.

For example: world war +1 (make sure there is a space between the + and the previous word).

The OR Operator

The OR operator allows you to search for pages that contain word A OR word B OR word C, etc. For example, to do a search on camping trips in either Yosemite or Yellowstone national parks, you would type the following: "camping trips" yosemite OR yellowstone

Combinations of Operators

To narrow your searches further, you can use combinations of search operators and phrase searches. Using our Atlanta Falcons example, typing "atlanta falcons" +nfl -"olympic games" -"birds of prey" will return a far higher proportion of relevant pages.

Numrange Searches

Numrange searches can be used to ensure that search results contain numbers within a specified range. You can conduct a numrange search by specifying two numbers, separated by two periods with no spaces.

For example, you would search for computers in the $600 to $900 price bracket by typing: computers $600..900

Numrange can be used for all types of units.

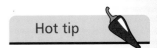

Hot tip

You may, at some stage, come across the phrase "Boolean Operators" with regard to search engines. These are derived from Boolean Logic, which is a system for establishing relationships between terms. The three main Boolean operators are:

- OR
- AND (equivalent to +)
- NOT (equivalent to -)

Hot tip

The most useful operators are: - (NOT) and quotation marks (phrase searching). These two operators can whittle a search result that would otherwise be several million pages down to a few hundred.

Repairing Internet Explorer

Internet Explorer is a highly complex piece of software and, as with Windows itself, it can over time become corrupted to the extent that it no longer works properly or little niggles and errors creep in.

The following applies to Internet Explorer 7 (bundled with Windows Vista).

Disable All Add-Ons

While browser add-ons can enhance your browsing, they do sometimes conflict with other software on your computer. To eliminate these as a possible source of the problem, try running Internet Explorer without any add-ons.

Do it by going to Start, All Programs, Accessories, System Tools, Internet Explorer (No Add-ons). If this resolves the problem, start Internet Explorer in the usual way (add-ons enabled) and then use the Add-ons Manager (Tools, Manage Add-ons, Enable or Disable Add-ons) to disable them one by one until the offender has been identified.

Reset Internet Explorer

If disabling add-ons doesn't solve the problem, try resetting Internet Explorer back to its default settings.

If Internet Explorer repeatedly stops responding, do the following:

• Scan the PC for malware

• Clear the contents of the Temporary Internet Files folder

Resetting Internet Explorer removes all changes that have been made to its settings since the time of its installation. It does not delete your Favorites and Feeds, though.

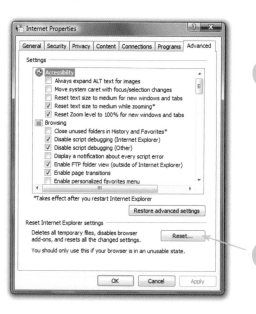

1. Open Internet Options in the Control Panel and click the Advanced tab

2. Click Reset...

10 Email

Email is one of the most popular and useful of all a computer's applications. It does, however, come with its own set of problems.

You Can't Send or Receive Email

The first thing to check is that your Internet connection is good. If your email facility has been working and then suddenly stops, this has to be the main suspect.

However, if you have just installed your email program, Windows itself or a program downloaded from the Internet, or the PC has just crashed, then misconfigured email settings are the most likely explanation.

Before you investigate these, though, check out your antivirus program (assuming you are running one). These programs check all emails – incoming and outgoing – and can be the cause of transmission or reception problems. Locate the antivirus program's Check Email function and disable it.

If this doesn't resolve the issue then your email settings are the next thing to check.

The simplest way to do this is to delete your email account and then set it up again. The following shows how it's done with Vista's Windows Mail:

Before you begin, you will need the information listed below (see margin note) to hand:

- The type of email server you use – POP3 (most email accounts), HTTP (services such as Hotmail), or IMAP

- The name of the incoming email server (usually POP)

- For POP3 and IMAP servers, the name of the outgoing email server (usually SMTP)

- Your account name (user name) and password

When you've got the information, do the following:

1 The first step is to delete your existing account. To do this, open Windows Mail and from the Tools Menu, click Accounts

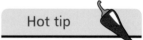

2 Select your email account and, on the right, click Remove. Then, in the same dialog box, click Add... This opens the New Account wizard

3 At the first screen, select E-mail Account

4 At the next screen, enter the name you want displayed in your outgoing messages

5 Enter your email address

Hot tip

While the setup procedure detailed here is specific to Windows Mail, the settings will be much the same whichever email application you are using.

In any case, all email programs will have an account setup wizard, which will help you to fill in all the required settings.

...cont'd

6 In the Incoming and Outgoing server boxes type POP and SMTP respectively, each followed by your ISP's address

To check that your email account is working, simply send yourself an email.

Alternatively, some email programs have a test facility that will check all the necessary settings and also send and receive a test email to confirm that everything is working correctly.

Set up e-mail servers

Incoming e-mail server type:

POP3

Incoming mail (POP3 or IMAP) server:

POP.ntlworld.com

Outgoing e-mail server (SMTP) name:

SMTP.ntlworld.com

☐ Outgoing server requires authentication

Where can I find my e-mail server information?

Next   Cancel

7 At the Internet Mail Logon screen, enter your user name and password

Hot tip

Checking the "Remember password" box in the Internet Mail Logon dialog box will eliminate the need to enter it manually each time you open your email program.

Internet Mail Logon

Type the account name and password your Internet service provider has given you.

E-mail username: Paul

Password: ••••••••••

☑ Remember password

Next   Cancel

Job done. You should now find that you can send and receive emails as before.

Email Attachments won't Open

You click a file attached to an email you've received but it refuses to open. The most likely explanation is that you don't have the necessary software installed on your PC with which to open the file. For example, a spreadsheet file created with Microsoft Excel will not open unless you have Excel on your system.

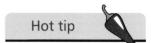
Hot tip

If you have a program on your PC that is capable of opening the attachment's file type, select the second option. Then browse to the program's location and select it. Windows will open the attachment with the program.

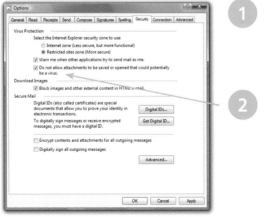

In this situation, Windows will give you a "Windows cannot open this file" error message as shown left.

Select the first option (see top margin note), which takes you to a site called cknow from where you will be able to identify the program used to create the file.

If you don't have the program on your PC, you will have to acquire and install it before you will be able to open the attachment.

This problem can also be caused by your Internet security settings. Check it out as follows:

Beware

Email attachments are the most common way of transmitting viruses. This is why Windows Mail and Outlook Express will refuse to open an attachment that contains a file type that is potentially dangerous. You disable this protection feature at your own risk.

1 From the Tools menu, click Options and the Security tab

2 Uncheck "Do not allow attachments to be saved or opened that could potentially be a virus"

Emails Take a Long Time to Download

The larger an email, the longer it will take to receive. Text messages are just a few KB in size and download in seconds; however, messages that contain media content (images, sound and video) can be several MB in size.

With a fast broadband connection this issue isn't too much of a problem, but with dial-up connections downloading large messages can take a long time, which is irritating.

The solution is to create a message rule that will prevent the download of any messages over a specified size.

1 Select Message Rules, Mail from the Tools menu. Check the "Where the message size is more than size" option, and in the next section, select "Do not Download it from the server"

New Mail Rule

Select your Conditions and Actions first, then specify the values in the Description.

1. Select the Conditions for your rule:
- [ ] Where the message is from the specified account
- [x] Where the message size is more than size
- [ ] Where the message has an attachment
- [ ] Where the message is secure

2. Select the Actions for your rule:
- [ ] Reply with message
- [ ] Stop processing more rules
- [x] Do not Download it from the server
- [ ] Delete it from server

3. Rule Description (click on an underlined value to edit it):

Apply this rule after the message arrives
Where the message size is more than size
Do not Download it from the server

4. Name of the rule:

New Mail Rule #1

Set Size

Set the size for your messages

Larger than: 50 KB

OK   Cancel

2 Under Rule Description, click "size", and in the box that opens enter the maximum message size that you will accept – see bottom margin note

Automatic Picture Resizing

As anybody who regularly uses email will know, email programs allow users either to insert images directly into the email or to attach them as files.

The problem with this is that unless the image has been reduced in size in an imaging program (a process of which many people are unsure), it is possible to end up sending a huge picture file that will take the recipient ages to download (see page 112).

Most people find this extremely irritating, as it can occupy their connection for a considerable length of time. The solution is to use the Windows Picture Resizing utility.

1 Right-click the image you want to send with your email, and select Send To and then Mail Recipient

2 Select the required option – Small, Medium, Original Size, etc – and then click Attach

3 Click OK and an email message window will open with the resized image attached. All you have to do is type in the address and the message text

A couple of things to be aware of are:

● Pictures resized in this way are converted to the JPEG format, which you may or may not want

● Some image formats cannot be converted by the utility, and thus cannot be resized. Such images will be attached to the email in their original size and format

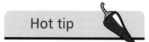

Hot tip

You can resize any number of pictures at the same time – you are not restricted to just one.

113

Beware

Be wary of using the Small and Smaller resizing options. While these reduce the size of files enormously, they also reduce the quality of the images considerably.

You Can't See Images in Emails

You receive an email that contains HTML (Internet) images but you are unable to see them. Instead, there is a white box where the images should be (with a little red X in the top-left corner), as shown below:

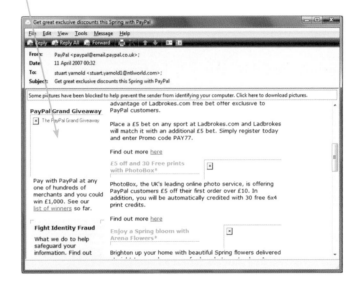

This is a security feature designed to protect users from the spammers.

To reveal the images, all you have to do is click the yellow information bar above the message. However, if you prefer to avoid bothering with this and to have the images open automatically, do the following:

1. From the Tools menu in Windows Mail or Outlook Express, click Options, Security

2. Uncheck "Block images and other external content in HTML e-mail"

Internet images will now open automatically. Before you do this, though, be sure you are aware of the possible ramifications – see margin notes.

Hot tip

Images that are contained in junk email messages frequently include web beacons that notify the sender's web server when you read or preview a message.

The web beacon validates your email address and will almost certainly result in you receiving more junk email and possibly viruses.

Hot tip

The image blocking feature also protects you from having to see offensive images.

Back Up Your Messages

Your email messages are stored in a file located in your user account folder. It's not uncommon for this file to become corrupt with the result that all your emails, both sent and received, vanish.

To guard against this possibility you should create a backup, as described below:

Windows Mail

1. Open Windows Mail

2. From the Tools menu, select Options, Advanced, Maintainance

3. Click Store Folder and the following dialog box will open

4. Here you will see the location of the folder containing your email file. Browse to the folder and simply copy its contents to a backup folder

Outlook Express

Open Outlook Express and from the Tools menu select Options, Maintenance. Click Store Folder and then follow the procedure as for Windows Mail.

In the event of losing your emails, all you have to do is copy the contents of the backup folder back to the Store Folder.

Hot tip

Instead of physically locating the Store Folder, just copy its address (shown in step 4) to the Run box (or the search box if you are using Windows Vista) on the Start Menu. Then click OK and the folder will open.

Beware

Don't forget that any emails sent or received after you make the backup will not be included in it. So create a backup regularly to keep it up to date.

Your Connection Closes Automatically

A common problem users experience with Outlook Express is the program automatically shutting down the Internet connection when it has finished sending and receiving messages. To rectify this, do the following:

1 Click Tools, Options and then the Connection tab. Uncheck the "Hang up..." box

Outlook Express Dials Automatically

This is another common problem and prevents users from being able to compose their messages offline. Fix it as follows:

1 On the Tools menu, click Options

2 Click the General tab and then uncheck "Send and receive messages at startup"

Your Inbox is Flooded with Spam

If you find yourself the recipient of an endless stream of advertisements, too-good-to-be-true offers, etc, what can you do about it?

The first step is to close your account and then set up a new one – this will stop it immediately. You then need to make sure the new account is kept out of the spammers' reach. Observing the following rules will help:

- Make your address as long as possible. Spammers use automated generators that churn out millions of combinations (aaa@aol.com, aab@aol.com, etc)

- Never post your address on a website. Spammers use spiders that trawl the web looking for the @ symbol, which is in all email addresses

- If you need to give an address to access a web page, give a false one. Alternatively, set up a specific account with filters that direct all received emails to the Deleted Items folder. Use this account when an address is asked for

- Never click the "Unsubscribe from this mailing list" link in a received email. This tells the spammer that your address is real, and could open the floodgates

- Make use of your email program's filters (message rules in Windows Mail and Outlook Express) – see page 118. Properly configured, these can cut out a lot of spam

- Use a Bayesian filter. This is available as a third-party product and integrates with your email program. Its effectiveness is due to the fact that it is "intelligent," and thus can be trained in much in the same way as voice recognition software. The Bayesian filter examines all aspects of a message, as opposed to simple keyword checking that classifies a message as spam on the basis of a single word or phrase. Once set up, a Bayesian filter will eliminate over 99% of spam

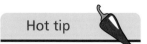

Hot tip

Once you are on the spammers' lists, the only way of stopping them is to close the account.

Beware

Chatrooms, Newsgroups and Message Boards are favorite places for spammers. Never post your email address on these sites.

Beware

Never reply to a spammer. If you do, you will confirm that your address is real.

...cont'd

Windows Mail and Outlook Express provide two utilities that will stop a large proportion of spam.

Message Rules

Also known as filters, message rules give the user a great deal of control over what makes it into the Inbox.

For example, the table below lists just some of the options provided by the Message Rules utility.

Conditions	Actions
Specific words in the message	Delete the message
Messages from specified accounts	Do not download from the server
Messages over a specified size	Delete from the server
Messages that contain attachments	Move to a specified folder
All messages	Reply with a message

Message rules can be accessed from Tools on the menu bar.

Blocked Senders List

This is a simple utility that is useful for blocking persistent emails from websites or an individual. To use it, right-click a message from the sender in question, select Junk E-mail and then "Add Sender to Blocked Senders List". From now on, Windows Mail or Outlook Express will automatically block all subsequent emails from the sender.

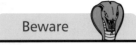

Beware

Be careful when creating rules to block emails. For example, if you create a rule to delete all messages containing specific words, a legitimate message that happens to contain one of those words will also be blocked. So rather than use single words, specify phrases.

Hot tip

The Blocked Senders list is useful for blocking emails from specific websites or individuals. Against spammers, however, who are constantly changing their addresses, it is much less effective.

11 Peripherals

On its own, there isn't much you can do with a basic computer. Peripheral devices are essential if you want to do something useful with it. In this chapter we look mainly at the two most popular peripherals – printers and scanners. We explain the most common faults and what to do about them.

Your Printer doesn't Work

When faced with this problem, the first thing to do is to ascertain whether the fault lies with the printer itself or with the computer. This is done by printing a test page.

Printer Test Page

All printers have the facility to print a test page, which is done with the printer isolated from the computer. Typically, this involves disconnecting the printer's interface cable from the computer and then pressing a combination of buttons – the procedure varies from printer to printer.

If this test is successful, it establishes that the printer itself is OK and that the fault is either software-related or with the connections. For instructions on how to carry out a printer test refer to your printer's documentation.

Check the Ink Levels and Nozzles

If the printer doesn't print the test page then you have a problem with the printer itself. Check the following:

- Is an ink cartridge empty? Most printer software will indicate the level of ink remaining

- Are the ink nozzles clear? Check by running the Head Cleaning utility

120

Vista users will find the Head Cleaning utility by opening Printers in the Control Panel. (This is called Printers and Faxes if you are running Windows XP.)

If the printer still doesn't work, it is faulty. Take it to a repair shop.

Printer Connections

Assuming the test page does print, the next thing to check is that the printer interface cable is OK and is connected to the correct port. It is very unlikely that there will be anything wrong with it but do check that the connection to both the printer and the PC is good.

Is The Printer Installed?

If there are no apparent problems with the printer's connections, you have a software issue. The first thing to check is that the device is installed correctly.

Go to Start, Control Panel and click Printers (Printers and Faxes if you are running Windows XP).

Beware

If you are using an old parallel port printer that is connected via another parallel port device, one may be preventing the other from working. Check this by connecting the printer directly to the computer.

1 If your printer is installed, it will be listed here

2 Make sure it is configured as the default printer. This is indicated by the check mark next to it. If it isn't, click the Printer icon and, from the Printer menu, click Set As Default Printer

If the printer isn't listed, its installation is corrupt.

Reinstall the device following the manufacturer's instructions.

Hot tip

If you have more than one printing device installed on the computer, it is quite possible that one of these has set itself as the default printer. Check this out in the Printers applet in the Control Panel.

...cont'd

Multiple Installations

A common cause of problems is the printer having been installed more than once. When faced with a printer that refuses to work, the first thing many people do is to reinstall it without checking to see if it actually needs to be reinstalled. When this happens, very often neither installation will work. If this is what you've done, delete (right-click and click Delete) all but one of the installations. See if the printer works now.

If it doesn't, and you have eliminated the printer and its connections as the cause of the fault and ascertained that it is correctly installed, you now know the problem is a configuration issue. Check the following.

Print Program

Establish that the fault isn't being caused by the program from which you are printing – your word processor for example. This is unlikely, it must be said, but it is a possibility. Check by trying a different program such as Notepad. Open it, type a few lines and see if the page prints.

If it does then the program you were using originally is faulty and needs to be re-installed.

Printer Settings

Check that the printer hasn't been "paused". You, or someone else, may have done this inadvertently.

 Go to Start, Control Panel, Printers. Click your printer and then click the Printer menu

EPSON Stylus Photo RX620 Series - Paused - Use Printer Offline

Printer Document View

	Status	Owner	Pages	Size	Sub
Connect					

✓ Set As Default Printer

Printing Preferences...

Update Driver

✓ Pause Printing

Cancel All Documents

Sharing...

✓ Use Printer Offline

Properties

Close

If the Pause Printing option has been selected, deselect it

Next, check the Windows Print Manager for non-responding print jobs.

1️⃣ Open a document (any one will do) and click Print. In the Notification Area, you will now see the Print Manager icon. Click to open it

2️⃣ Right-click the print job and click Cancel

EPSON Stylus Photo RX620 Series						
Printer Document View						
Document Name	Status	Owner	Pages	Size		Sub
Microsoft Word - DipDEA Quali.			57/58	1.92 MB/2.01 ...		13:
	Pause					
	Restart					
	Cancel					
Cancels the selected documents.	Properties					

When the print job has been cancelled (this can take a while), try the print process again.

If there is still no joy, check the spool file. This is a buffer to which all print jobs are sent for queuing (this speeds up the printing process). Problems with the spool file can prevent the printer from working.

Check this by opening your printer software as previously described, and selecting the "Print directly to the printer" option.

Printing is Slow

If a document is being printed at a lower than normal speed, the most likely cause is that it contains graphics, which can be enormous in size. If the computer's memory isn't large enough to cope with the volume of data being sent to it, or is already occupied by other applications, printing speed will be compromised.

If this is a one-off situation it isn't too much of a problem, but if you print many graphic-rich documents you may want to try the following:

- Decrease the size of any graphics in the document

- Increase the amount of available memory

Taking the former first, there are two ways to reduce the size of images included in a print file.

First, reduce their resolution and color depth. This is easily achieved with an imaging program such as Irfanview.

Second, save the image in a low-size image format such as JPEG. This can also be done in the same imaging program.

With regard to memory, you must increase the amount that is available to the printing operation. The best way to do this is to switch the PC off and back on, which will clear its memory. Also, don't have any other programs running while printing is in progress.

If you carry out both of the above steps you should have no printing speed problems unless your machine is seriously underspecified to begin with. In this case, you will need to upgrade its components, memory in particular.

If the required print quality is not high, you can speed up printing by selecting a low-quality print setting in the printer software.

Hot tip

If you do, or plan to do, a lot of image-intensive printing and you are having problems with your existing setup, a memory upgrade will perform wonders as regards printing speed.

Print Quality is Poor

Blocked Print Nozzles

Typical symptoms are gaps or faint areas in the printed document, poor quality color, white horizontal lines and even no print output at all.

The cause on an inkjet printer is that the nozzles have become blocked, or partially blocked, by dried ink. Blocked nozzles are likely to be encountered in printers which haven't been used for a while. You can prevent this by using the printer regularly, even if it's only to print a few words every other day.

If the symptoms do indicate blocked nozzles, run the Nozzle Check and Head Cleaning utilities from the printer software. These will be found under the Utility or Maintenance tab.

Use the Nozzle Check utility to confirm that the problem is blocked nozzles

Use the Head Cleaning utility to clean the nozzles

Keep the Printer Clean

Allowing the printer to get dirty is guaranteed to adversely affect the quality of your printed documents eventually. Although the print quality itself won't be affected, it can detract from the finished document in the form of smudges and streaks.

Use a brush or a can of compressed air to clear away general dust and dirt from the inner workings of the printer.

Hot tip

Another good reason for using your inkjet printer regularly is that many of them will automatically run the Nozzle Cleaning utility after a prolonged period of inactivity.

The problem with this is that the nozzle cleaning process uses a considerable amount of ink. As inkjet cartridges are anything but cheap you don't want to be wasting ink in this fashion.

Hot tip

Sometimes, if the nozzles are severely blocked, you will find you may need to run the Head Cleaning utility several times before the print quality is up to scratch. This is another good reason to use the printer regularly.

...cont'd

Another cause of spoiled print output is the Nozzle Cleaning utility, which works by forcing ink through the nozzles to clear them. It's not uncommon for the printer's platen to become contaminated with ink by this. The ink will then be transferred to the document, causing unsightly streaks. If this happens you will have to clean the ink off the platen with a suitable solvent.

Printer Software Settings

Yet another cause of low quality printing is the selection of unsuitable settings in the printer software. For example, choosing economy print resolution (about 180 dpi) will result in a faint print output.

For high quality printing you need 720 dpi or above. The drawback is that the higher the dpi setting, the slower the print speed. Also, the printer will use a lot more ink.

Hot tip

Platen contamination is rare with modern printers but is common with models a few years old.

Don't forget

Before printing, you need to select the correct type of paper for the particular application. When printing photos, for example, you need to use photo-quality glossy paper.

For good quality printing you need to select suitable settings in the printer software

Tell the printer what type of paper you are using

Using the wrong type of paper can also cause problems. For example, you need to use special glossy paper for printing high quality photos. Also, it's no good choosing the right kind of paper and then hoping the printer will correctly guess what it is – it won't. You need to select it in the printer software as shown above.

Inkjet Cartridge Refills

Branded inkjet cartridges are extremely expensive and because of this a whole industry has developed in which companies can seriously undercut the printer manufacturers' prices and still show a profit. However, many people have had unhappy results with ink refill kits and the jury still appears to be out as to their worth.

Pros

The main advantage of these kits is the price – a typical kit costs about the same as a branded cartridge while offering about five times the amount of ink.

Another plus is convenience – if your cartridge gives up in the middle of the night and you have to get the document finished by morning, supplies will be at hand.

Cons

Most of these kits involve injecting the ink into the cartridge with a syringe. As many people have discovered, this can be a very messy business indeed. It is also not uncommon for the refilled cartridge to leak while in use. This can result in a constant need for printer cleaning.

Using any old ink will not do – inks need to be formulated according to the brand of cartridge. Put the wrong type of ink in your cartridge and it might well not work at all. There is also the issue of ink quality. Predictably, the printer manufacturers claim that the quality of ink supplied with refill kits is inferior to their own and this is undoubtedly true in many cases. However, due to the huge profits to be made in the inkjet market, many reputable companies have been set up and these do supply a quality product. The problem is identifying them.

It is a fact, though, that millions of people are now using these kits and the consensus seems to be that as long as you use a kit from a reputable supplier you will get good results.

Just don't forget to use a lot of newspaper when refilling your cartridge.

Hot tip

If you don't wish to get your hands dirty, you can take your empty cartridges to specialist stores where the cartridge will be filled for you.

Hot tip

Inkjet cartridge print heads have a limited lifespan. Even if you can refill your cartridge successfully, you will eventually have to junk it and buy a new one. The time to do this will be when your print quality becomes unacceptable.

Your Scanner doesn't Work

Scanners are essentially simple devices with little to go wrong inside them. If yours doesn't work, the following are most likely causes.

Scanner Initialization Failure

You attempt to scan a document or image but get a "Scanner initialization failed", "Scanner not found" or similar error message, as shown below.

This can indicate several things: the scanner is faulty, the scanner driver is corrupt, or there is a poor connection.

The first thing to check is the connections:

1. Close the scanner software

2. Disconnect the scanner from the computer

3. Disconnect the scanner's power cable

4. Turn the computer off and then turn it on again

5. Reconnect the scanner's power cable

6. Reconnect the scanner to the computer (use a different port on the computer if possible)

If the scanner still doesn't work, go to the next step.

Check the Scanner

Test the scanner itself by using the following procedure.

Disconnect the interface and power cables from the scanner and then reconnect them. The carriage on the scanner will move forward and then backward (this will be audible). Also, the internal light will come on.

If neither of these things happens, you have a faulty scanner. Return it to the manufacturer for repair or replacement.

A Corrupt or Missing Driver

Check this out in the Device Manager.

If your scanner is installed it will be listed under "Imaging devices". If so, the problem is likely to be a bad connection to the computer.

However, if it's not, or you don't see an "Imaging devices" category, the driver is missing or corrupt. Install or reinstall the device from the installation disc.

Hot tip

Something for those of you with a USB scanner to be aware of is that USB requires a driver to enable it to function. So if you get a "Scanner not found" error message when you attempt a scan, this is something else for you to check.

Open the Device Manager, and at the bottom you will see a "Universal Serial Bus controllers" category. Any problems with your USB driver will be indicated here.

Should you need to reinstall the USB driver, you will find it on the motherboard installation disc.

Scanning is Slow

First, it must be said that there are scanners and then there are scanners. Some operate much more quickly than others so establish that yours isn't one of the slowcoaches before ripping it apart or taking it back to the store. Reading a few reviews of your model on the Internet should provide some clues.

Hot tip

Setting the scan resolution to 300 dpi or less will keep the image file small and so speed up the scanning process.

If you experience an abnormally slow scan, though, the usual reason is that the image or document is being scanned at too high a resolution. This means the scan heads are having to read large amounts of data, which will of course slow the scan speed. Resolve this as follows.

In the scanner software, lower the scan resolution. 300 dpi is more than enough for most applications. In some cases, even that is overkill.

Hot tip

If you are scanning an image for use in a web page, use a resolution of 72 dpi and save the image as a JPEG.

Setting the scan resolution to 300 dpi or less will keep the image file small and so speed up the scanning process. The table below shows what scan resolutions to use for typical applications

Application	Resolution
Images for commercial printing	300 dpi
Images to be enlarged	1200 dpi upwards
Photos for printing on inkjet printers	300 dpi
Text documents	300 dpi
Line art (drawings, diagrams, etc)	300 dpi
Images for websites	72 dpi

Scanned Files are Slow to Open

This is another result of scanning at too high a resolution, which results in a larger than necessary (sometimes huge) file size. All the file's data has to be loaded into the computer's memory and, as a result, it is slow to open.

The solution is to rescan the document, this time at a lower resolution. The second scan will look the same as the first, but the file size will be much smaller.

To illustrate this point, a page of text scanned in at 300 dpi results in a file approximately 900 KB in size while the same page scanned at 600 dpi gives a file size of some 3.5 MB – nearly four times as big. However, in terms of clarity, the two scans will be virtually indistinguishable.

Another cause can be a system low in memory. If for some reason you must scan at the highest possible resolution, you may find that you have to upgrade your system in terms of memory capacity.

Also remember that having other applications running at the same time as the file is being opened reduces the amount of memory available to the computer, thus slowing things down.

Scanned Images are Not Accurate

Sometimes a scanned image looks somewhat different from the original picture – it might be a lot darker, for example. This is caused by an inherent weakness found in many scanners – poor Gamma translation.

Gamma is the term used as a measure of the brightness of mid-level tones in an image.

The problem can be corrected by using the Gamma Correction control found in any good imaging program, such as Irfanview (see www.irfanview.com).

Hot tip

A phenomenon known as Moiré can be an issue when scanning a newspaper or magazine photograph. This manifests itself as a herringbone pattern of interference. Most scanner software will have a Moiré control (sometimes called Descreening).

...cont'd

Image before correction   Image after correction

Gamma correction control in Irfanview

Garbled or Missing Text

When a scanned text document is imported into a word processor, it first needs to go through a process known as Optical Character Recognition (OCR). This converts the image file into a text file that the word processor can recognise. OCR programs are supplied with all scanners.

Unfortunately OCR software doesn't always produce perfect results – it makes the occasional mistake. While good OCR software can be 99% accurate, this will still result in several errors on any one page of text.

This is the first thing to be aware of – it isn't a fault as such, but rather the result of a technology that hasn't been perfected yet.

The performance of any OCR program basically comes down to the clarity of the text being scanned in.

The more defined the text is, i.e. dark characters on a white background, the better the result. Similarly, small characters will be more difficult for the OCR program to read accurately. Also, the characters must be uniform – handwritten text will produce nothing but gibberish.

Part of a Scanned Document is Missing

All scanner software includes a Preview mode, which allows you to select the part of the image you want to scan. If, after the scan has completed, you find that a required part of your image is missing, it will be because you have cropped it out during the preview stage.

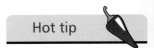

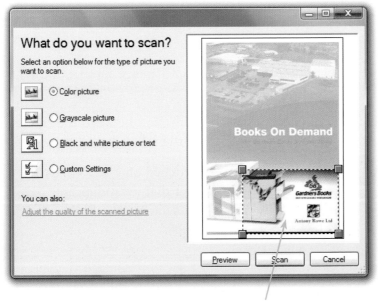

In this example, only the part of the document within the rectangle will be scanned

Rescan the document and this time make sure all of it is included in the scan.

133

Digital Camera Issues

Digicams, as they are commonly known, are very popular devices and sales of them now far outstrip those of traditional film cameras.

This is because users are able to see their pictures immediately and also subsequently edit them on their computers. However, the latter can only be done if you can get the pictures into the computer in the first place. This potential problem is what we'll look at first.

Pictures Won't Download to the PC

When you connect the camera to the PC, you have one of the following problems:

- The camera is not listed as an available device in My Computer

- You get an error message such as "The computer cannot detect the scanner or camera" or "No Image Capture device connected"

- Errors occur when you transfer image files from the camera to the computer

These all indicate either no connection between the camera and the PC, or a poor one. Do the following:

1. Check the camera is switched on – if it isn't, the PC won't see it. (Don't forget that most digicams have a power saving mode that switches the device off after a few minutes of inactivity.)

2. Some cameras must be set to the image viewing mode in order to be detected by the computer. Check that you have done this

3. Check that the USB transfer cable is connected to both the camera and the PC

Hot tip

Before a digital camera will download pictures to a computer it must be switched on. Don't overlook this obvious step. Also, some cameras need to be set to a specific mode before they can communicate with Windows. Check your camera documentation to confirm this if you are unsure.

Hot tip

Windows XP and Windows Vista both provide native USB support. However, it may not be compatible with your digicam's software. If this is the case, you may need to download an update to the software from the manufacturer's website.

4 Connect the USB cable to a different USB socket on the PC (it is possible for a USB socket to be faulty)

5 If the USB cable is connected to a USB hub, bypass the hub by connecting it directly to the PC

6 If the camera is the first USB device you have used with the PC, it is possible that USB is not enabled in the BIOS. Correct this as follows:

1) Go into the PC's BIOS setup program (see page 37)

2) Using the arrow keys, scroll down to Integrated Peripherals. Press Enter and scroll to Onchip PCI Device

3) Press Enter again and you will see the Onchip USB Controller option. Enable it, save the change and exit the BIOS

7 Your camera may require a driver to be installed in order for the computer to detect the camera. Install the driver according the manufacturer's instructions (also, check the manufacturer's website for an updated driver)

If you still can't get a connection to the PC, there is a fault with either the camera, the camera's memory card or the USB cable.

The first one to check is the USB cable. Do this by trying a different one. Then replace the memory card. If you still can't get a connection, the camera has to be faulty.

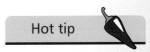

Hot tip

If you have a memory card reader, you can use this to transfer the images to the computer. This will isolate the cause of the problem to either the camera or the memory card.

...cont'd

Hot tip

Use of a tripod will eliminate camera motion completely but isn't always practical.

Beware

Be aware that the more you zoom in to a scene, the more pronounced the effect of camera motion. This applies particularly with low-end cameras. In this situation, it may be necessary to use a tripod.

Problems with Your Pictures

Having got your pictures onto your PC, you may find that they don't look quite as good as you expected. The following are the most common problems.

Images are Blurred

There are three causes of blurred pictures:

- Camera motion
- Subject motion
- Incorrect focus

This problem is most pronounced with cheaper digicams, which tend to have slow shutter speeds. To avoid camera motion, you must hold the camera as steady as possible while taking the shot. The best way to do this is to use the viewfinder (assuming there is one) to compose the shot (it is harder to hold the camera steady when you have it out at arm's length and are using the LCD).

If there is motion in the scene being snapped, you must either use the appropriate preset setting – see your camera documentation – or manually select a faster shutter speed (assuming this option is available).

The other possibility is that the subject is out of focus. The best way around this problem is to let your camera "prefocus" on your subject by holding the shutter control halfway down for a moment before taking the shot.

Pixelated or Grainy Images

If your pictures have a blocky, pixelated appearance, the reason will be that the camera is set to a low-resolution mode. Locate the setting that allows you to change the resolution and set it to a higher level.

The drawback with doing this is that the higher the resolution, the larger the size of each picture file. This in turn means that the camera's memory card will have room for fewer pictures.

Another common problem is noise – this gives images a grainy look. This is caused by using too high an ISO value (this is the measurement of the camera's sensitivity to light).

A high ISO lets you use faster shutter speeds and smaller apertures, but at the cost of noise. Most cameras use an automatic ISO setting that will change as necessary. Typically, this setting will avoid the noisier ISO values. However, if it does not, you will have to set the ISO manually as detailed in the camera's documentation.

Images Are Under- or Over-Exposed

If *all* your images suffer from this problem, the cause is probably not the camera, but simply that the brightness control on your monitor is incorrectly adjusted.

If the problem is peculiar to your indoor shots, or outside shots taken at night, and they're all under-exposed, then either you haven't used the camera's flash or the scene was beyond the effective range of the flash. Note that digicams typically have a maximum flash range of about nine feet.

If parts of outdoor or complex scenes are too dark or light, the usual cause is that the prevailing lighting conditions have misled the camera's light meter into under- or over-exposing the shot.

One solution to this is to use the camera's flash fill mode to illuminate the dark sections of a scene. However, as we mentioned above, flash guns have a limited range so it will have to be a close-up shot for this to be effective.

A better way to is simply to adjust the direction from which you take the shot so that the light source is behind you rather than the subject. Remember, when the light source is behind your subject it will appear too dark, almost like a silhouette.

Hot tip

Images have much more noise in shadowy sections. If you've under-exposed an image and then tried to make it look right on the computer, it will often have a grainy appearance.

Hot tip

Dark scenes, such as those taken at night, are more likely to be grainy, as the camera will have to use a higher ISO setting.

137

...cont'd

Hot tip

As a general rule, presets, while producing decent results, are never as good as a manually set up camera.

Hot tip

Taking the time to read the camera's documentation, to learn what the various controls do, will enable you to take much better photographs.

Poor Color

Color is the most difficult element of a picture to get right with digicams and there are several reasons for this.

The main cause of color problems is incorrect white balance. White balance is a means of calibrating a camera to record true white correctly. All other colors produced by the camera are based on the white balance. So if the camera's white balance is incorrect, all other colors will also be incorrect.

Digital cameras are set to automatic white balance by default and this does a very good job under most circumstances. However, there are times when the white balance needs to be changed manually to match the prevailing lighting conditions in order to obtain more true-to-life colors in a photo.

To this end, most digital cameras provide a range of white balance presets – typically Tungsten, Daylight, Cloudy, Flash and Shade. These enable the user to instruct the camera how to handle the lighting conditions.

However, while results are reasonable, they are never optimal. If you are serious about your digital photography, to get the best out of your pictures in terms of color you need to set the white balance manually. It is beyond the scope of this book to explain this subject but you will find many websites and books that provide full instructions.

Imaging Software

Programs such as Photoshop and Paintshop Pro can be used to correct many common image defects – incorrect exposure, blur, and color casts are typical examples.

However, there is no substitute for getting the image right first time, and if you take advantage of the many controls provided with even the cheapest digital cameras you should rarely have to use an imaging program.

The Mouse doesn't Work

The cause of this problem depends on what type of mouse you are using.

If it is the old-fashioned mechanical ball and wheel type, you almost certainly have a bad connection to the PC – there's little else to go wrong.

Check that the cable is connected to the green PS/2 mouse port at the rear of the computer. Note that the purple connection below, which is otherwise identical, is for the keyboard. It is very easy to connect the mouse to this port by mistake.

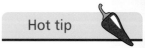

Hot tip

If the mouse uses the PS/2 port, you must switch the PC off before unplugging it or plugging it in. USB mice, however, can be connected with the PC running.

If the mouse is a USB model, try connecting it to a different USB socket.

If you are using an optical mouse (this will have a flashing LED on the underside, as shown below), the problem could be a connection issue as above. If it's a battery-operated cordless model, it could also be that the batteries have run out.

LED

139

Another possibility with cordless mice is that the radio frequency connection between the mouse and its receiver has been lost. Resolve this by removing the batteries from the mouse and then replacing them. This action will automatically reinstate the radio connection (note that you may also have to press a button on the mouse or the receiver – see the mouse documentation).

You should also be aware that cordless mice have a limited range – typically about nine feet or so.

Mouse Operation is Poor

Poor mouse operation can mean slow, intermittent or erratic movement of the pointer.

With a mechanical ball and wheel mouse, the problem will be due to a build-up of dirt on the internal wheels. Open the device and simply scrape the dirt away. The mouse will then be as good as new.

If you are using an optical mouse, use a cotton swab or cotton cleaning bud to clean the plastic LED covering. Any dirt here may inhibit correct operation of the LED and the associated sensor.

Batteries that are about to die will also cause this problem.

If cleaning does not resolve the issue, you may have a virus. Run a virus check on your system. If you still have problems, try the mouse on a different computer.

12 Security

These days computer users face an unprecedented barrage of threats to their data. In this chapter we see what these are and how to deal with them.

Viruses – an Overview

Hot tip

A virus definition list is simply an updated list of the most recent viruses to be discovered. Without this list, your program, no matter how good, cannot be relied upon to keep your system clean of viruses.

A virus is a computer program that can copy itself and infect a computer without the permission or knowledge of the user. There are many different types of virus but the one thing they all have in common is that they compromise or even destroy the functionality of the affected computer.

Some viruses are programmed to damage computers by corrupting programs, deleting files, or reformatting the hard drive. Others are more benign and simply replicate themselves, and perhaps make their presence known by presenting text, video, or audio messages.

However, even these benign viruses can cause problems. For example, they take up computer memory used by legitimate programs and, as a result, they often cause erratic behavior and even system crashes. Also, many viruses are bug-ridden, and these bugs may lead to system crashes and data loss.

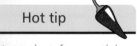

Hot tip

Note that free antivirus programs will never be as good, or well featured, as the ones you have to pay for. However, for occasional use they are quite adequate.

Virtually all viruses these days are transmitted via the Internet, so if you never use this medium the issue of viruses is not one that you need to concern yourself with very much. Just remember that viruses can also be transmitted via floppy disks and CDs/DVDs, so if you run one of these acquired from an unverifiable source, you should scan it first.

However, if you do use the Internet you will need to have an antivirus program running whenever you are connected to it. Most people are aware of this; what many aren't aware of is that the antivirus program's definitions list (see top margin note) needs to be updated on a regular basis so that the program can detect the latest viruses.

Hot tip

Free antivirus programs are available at www.avast.com, www.pandasoftware. com and www. activevirusshield.com.

Most of the latest antivirus programs do this automatically but some don't so you need to check your program out in this respect.

If you only use the Internet occasionally it may not be worth the expense of buying an antivirus program. Instead, visit one of the websites from which you can download free programs, or run online checks – see bottom margin note.

Dealing with a Virus

The first thing is to be sure that you do actually have a virus. The following are the most common indicators:

- Spontaneous system reboots

- System or application crashes or hang-ups

- Corrupted hard drive data

- System slowdowns

- Your computer tries to connect to the Internet

- New icons appear on the Desktop

- Your computer has less available memory than it should

If your PC displays any of the above symptoms, do the following:

1. If you have an antivirus program, make sure its virus definitions list is up to date

2. Scan the PC with the antivirus program. If you don't have one, use one of the free programs available on the Internet

3. If the scan identifies a virus, follow the program's instructions to get rid of it

4. If the program is unable to delete the virus, reboot the PC into Safe Mode (see page 35) and run the scan again; this will often do the trick. If this doesn't work either, visit the program manufacturer's website and see if there is a utility written specifically for the virus

5. In the unlikely event that the virus is still present, you have two choices:
   - take the PC to a repair shop
   - reformat the hard drive and then reinstall Windows and your applications

Don't forget

All the major manufacturers of antivirus programs have lists of common viruses and their symptoms available for perusal on their websites.

143

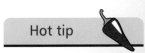

Hot tip

Some viruses need a specially written utility to uninstall them. These are available from the antivirus manufacturers' websites.

Malware

A relatively recent phenomenon, which is due in large part to the explosion in broadband connections, is malware. This is a term that encompasses invasive software such as adware, spyware and browser hijackers, which are downloaded to users' PCs without their knowledge.

Quite apart from compromising your PC's security and intruding on your privacy, they can also slow your Internet activities considerably and, in the case of browser hijackers, can have a drastic impact on the PC's performance.

Users of Windows Vista are protected against programs of this type by a built-in anti-malware program called Windows Defender. This automatically scans the PC at regular intervals and uninstalls any malware that it finds.

However, users of Windows XP do not have this protection, and so must always be on their guard. To check your PC for the existence of malware, go to www.lavasoft.com and download a free copy of Ad-aware. This program will detect and delete most malware.

Having got your system clean, keep it so by avoiding the following activities:

- Downloading freeware and shareware programs from the Internet

- Browsing the Internet with any of Internet Explorer's security features turned off

- Installing software from unverifiable sources

If you are running Windows XP, install Service Pack 2 and also download the latest version of Internet Explorer (currently version 7) from the Microsoft website. Both of these upgrades contain more advanced security tools designed specifically to combat malware and browser hijackers.

Hot tip

Classic indicators of malware include:

- The appearance of toolbars in your browser

- A noticeable slowing down of your Internet connection

- Pop-up windows

- Your browser crashing

- Sites added to your Favorites list

Hot tip

No anti-malware program is perfect, so to ensure your system is as clean as possible, we suggest you also use Spybot Search & Destroy (available from www.safer-networking.org).

144

Browser Hijackers

In its simplest form, browser hijacking is when a program changes your browser's home page (the one it goes to initially when the browser is opened) to a different one.

Many ISPs do this and all you have to do is go to Internet Options in the Control Panel, open the General tab and change the home page back to the one you prefer.

However, malicious hijackers do not allow you to undo the change, and so every time you open your browser you are taken to a website of their choice, usually one containing advertising or pornography.

Other symptoms include toolbars added to your browser and redirection of your web searches. In the worst cases, your browser is taken over completely and will only go to sites that the hijacker wants you to visit (again, usually advertising and pornography sites).

These programs can be very difficult to remove and doing so requires a level of knowledge that the typical user just doesn't have. The solution is to scan your PC with one of the specialist anti-hijacking programs written specifically to combat them.

While the anti-malware programs mentioned on the previous page will catch many of these hijackers, they are not effective against the more virulent ones. To get rid of these you need HijackThis and CWShredder, both of which are available at www.merijn.org.

Even if your system is currently clear of browser hijackers, we recommend you download these two programs and keep them on your PC. One of the tricks employed by hijacking programs is to prevent you accessing the websites of anti-hijacking program manufacturers, thus making it impossible to download the programs when they are needed.

To prevent the unintentional download of a hijacker, you should update your browser to Internet Explorer 7, or install Mozilla's Firefox browser.

Beware

Some hijackers actually prevent you installing anti-hijacking programs. They can also remove access to Internet Options and the PC's registry so that you have no way of uninstalling them.

Furthermore, even if you do manage to uninstall them, they will simply reinstall themselves from a separate file hidden on the PC.

Hot tip

One of the worst browser hijackers is the notorious coolwebsearch. The CWShredder program has been written specifically to deal with this hijacker.

Firewalls

A firewall is a hardware device or a software program that blocks the unauthorized transmission of data between a computer and a network (the main network being the Internet). It also logs attempted intrusions.

This type of protection is absolutely essential when a PC is connected to the Internet, particularly if it is using an always-on broadband connection.

If you don't use a firewall, you leave yourself open to the risk of a hacker (using specialized software) gaining access to your computer. The hacker can place malicious software on your machine, steal private data such as passwords and email addresses, and use your computer to attack other computers.

If you are using Windows XP and haven't installed Service Pack 2, you almost certainly don't have a firewall enabled. While XP does provide a firewall, it is disabled by default. If this is the situation, enable it as follows:

1. Go to Start, Control Panel, Network Connections

2. Right-click your connection and click Properties

3. Open the Advanced tab and check the "Protect My Computer..." checkbox

If you have installed Service Pack 2 the firewall will be enabled by default. However, you should be aware that XP's firewall only prevents data entering the computer – it doesn't prevent data leaving it. So, for example, if you have a spyware program on your PC, it will be able to send data to its owner regardless of the fact that the firewall is running.

For this reason we suggest that you download Zone Alarm (a free firewall from www.zonealarm.com) and use that instead. This offers both incoming and outgoing protection.

The firewall provided with Windows Vista is enabled by default and offers both incoming and outgoing protection.

Hot tip

It is much more important to have a firewall active when you have a permanent broadband connection.

Hot tip

Firewalls are also available as hardware devices, and are usually built in to network hardware such as routers. These are more efficient than software firewalls.

146

Securing Your Data

Your data is vulnerable to two kinds of attacker:

- Someone with physical access to your PC

- Someone with remote access to your PC, e.g. a hacker or a spyware programmer

The simplest way to prevent unauthorized physical access is to password-protect your account. Do this as follows:

Hot tip

There is also the issue of physical theft of the PC. To this end there are various security systems available to prevent thieves simply tucking PCs under their arms and walking away with them.

1 Go to Start, Control Panel, User Accounts

2 If you are running Windows XP, click "Change an account" and click the desired account. Then click "Create a password"

3 If you are running Windows Vista, click "Create a password for your account"

4 Enter and confirm your password

...cont'd

Set a Boot Password

Another method is to set a boot password. Most BIOS setup programs provide an option to password-protect the bootup procedure. To do this, start the PC and enter the BIOS setup program.

On the opening screen you will see an option to "Set User Password". Select this and enter a password; this password-protects the BIOS setup program itself. Then look for a security option (often found on the Advanced BIOS Features page). This enables you to set a boot password. Do so, save the changes and exit the BIOS. Now bootup will stop at the boot screen and ask you to enter the password.

In the case of remote access, while the PC may have been infiltrated you can still protect sensitive data – website usernames and passwords, credit card details, etc – by keeping it in a password-protected folder. A hacker will have to crack the password to access the data in the file and most won't bother – they'll seek an easier target.

The simplest way to do this with Windows XP is to create a compressed folder. Do this by right-clicking the Desktop, click New and then click Compressed (zipped) Folder. Place your data in the compressed folder and then, from the File menu, click Add a Password.

With Windows Vista, this is more difficult as the password feature has been removed from compressed folders. The simplest option here is to download a program called Private Folder 1.0 from the Internet (do a Google search for it). This program was written by Microsoft and, while it is no longer supported by them, it is widely available and offers a good solution.

Hot tip

There are many other password protection programs available on the Internet, many of them free. However, Microsoft's Private Folder 1.0 is the one we recommend.

Keep Your Activities Private

You have been doing something on the PC that you wish to keep private. How can you do this? The main giveaways are the following:

The Internet

We'll start with the Internet. Internet Explorer keeps a record of your browsing activities in three places:

- The Temporary Internet Files folder
- The History folder
- The Cookies folder

If necessary, you can delete these records as follows:

1 Go to Start, Control Panel, Internet Options

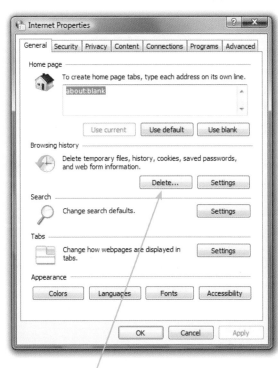

2 Under "Browsing history", click Delete…

If you are using Windows XP, you will have separate Delete buttons for each folder.

Hot tip

Each time you access the Internet, a new set of browsing records is created.

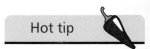
Hot tip

You can configure Internet Explorer to delete the contents of the Temporary Internet Files folder automatically when it is closed. You will find this option on the Advanced tab in the Internet Options utility in the Control Panel.

Hot tip

Mozilla's Firefox browser can be configured to delete all traces of your browsing activities automatically when it is closed.

...cont'd

Hot tip

Get rid of the
Frequently Used
Programs list
permanently as
described below:

1) Right-click the
   Taskbar and click
   Properties
2) Click the Start
   Menu tab
3) Uncheck "Store
   and display a list
   of recently opened
   programs"

Hot tip

Hide XP's My Recent
Documents list as
follows:

1) Right-click the
   Taskbar and select
   Properties
2) Click the Start
   Menu tab and then
   click Customize
3) Click the Advanced
   tab
4) Uncheck the "List
   my most recently
   opened documents"
   checkbox

Programs Run

A feature found in both XP and Vista is the Frequently Used Programs list. This list updates automatically according to the frequency with which programs are run.

If a program that you don't want others to know you have been using is on this list, right-click it and click "Remove from this list". However, it may well reappear with subsequent usage so this is not an ideal solution (see the margin note for a permanent solution).

Files

With Windows Vista there is a Recent Items list on the Start Menu. This displays the 15 most recently opened files on the

computer and is one of the most obvious indications of what a user has been doing.

You can disable it as described below:

① Right-click the Taskbar and click Properties. Then click the Start Menu tab

② Uncheck "Store and display a list of recently opened files"

Windows XP has a My Recent Documents link on the Start Menu. As with Vista's Recent Items list, this displays a list of recently accessed files. You can hide this as described in the bottom margin note.

User Account Control (UAC)

User Account Control is a new security feature in Vista that displays a "need permission" window when a user wants to do certain actions, e.g. install a program or a device driver.

These requests are extremely intrusive and, because of this, the first thing most users are going to do is disable the feature. However, before they do, they should be aware of what UAC actually does and the reason for it being there.

There are two types of user account in Vista: administrator accounts that have unlimited rights, and standard accounts that have restrictions (limited rights) placed on them. Because an administrative account has access to every feature of the operating system, any malicious software that is installed on that account will also have access to everything. This means it can do unlimited damage. Malicious software on a standard account is limited in the same way as the account holder is, so the potential for damage is much less.

What UAC does is to run an administrator account with the same privileges as a standard account, i.e. limited, until an action that requires administrator privileges is initiated. This is when the "need permission" window will pop up. If the user approves the request with a physical mouse click, the account temporarily switches to full administrator privileges until the action has been carried out. It then reverts back to the standard mode.

Therefore, as a malicious program is unable to operate the mouse, there is nothing it can do. However, there could still be the danger of the program tricking the user into approving an action he or she shouldn't by presenting a spoof dialog box – see margin note. This leads us to the Secure Desktop.

This feature disables the Desktop (you'll see it darken when this happens) when an action that requires permission is being carried out. In this situation, only trusted Windows processes are allowed to run – third-party applications (including malicious software) are blocked. Thus, a malicious program is unable to present a spoof dialog box.

Hot tip

All administrator accounts are actually run as standard accounts most of the time. They only get administrator status when it is needed.

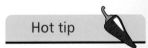

Hot tip

Hackers use software that present spoof dialog boxes. When a button is clicked, they carry out a malicious action rather than the safe one the user was expecting. In this way, they can bypass a PC's security measures.

...cont'd

The most obvious manifestations of UAC are the "need permission" dialog boxes (an example is shown below) that pop up when the user trys to perform certain actions – installing a program, for example – and the Secure Desktop (when access to the Desktop is removed) is activated.

For users who decide they can live without this (most people, we suspect), the solution is as follows:

Beware

You should disable UAC only if you are aware of the security issues involved. It is there for a reason.

1. Go to Start, Control Panel, User Accounts. Click "Turn User Account Control on or off"

2. Uncheck "Use User Account Control (UAC) ..."

13 Files and Folders

In this chapter we examine a range of problems experienced when handling files and folders.

You are Unable to Delete a File

You right-click a file and click Delete but it refuses to go. There are several possible causes for this behavior but the most common one is that the file is in use. In this situation you will get an error message as shown below.

File In Use	X
⚠	The action can't be completed because the file is open in another program
	Close the file and try again.
	fwinstall.exe Date created: 09/04/2007 14:48 Size: 0 bytes
	Try Again Cancel

The first thing is to close any program that is obviously open – these will be indicated on the Taskbar. Then try deleting the file again.

If it still won't go and you have no idea which program it is open in, the easiest solution is to reboot the computer. This will close all running programs on the computer. On restart, you should be able to delete the file.

However, there are situations in which even this won't work. In this case, reboot the computer into Safe Mode as described on page 35. In the vast majority of cases, you will then be able to delete the file. Then reboot back into the normal Windows mode.

In the unlikely event that the file still refuses to go, it has almost certainly been created by a virus. Run your antivirus program to get rid of it.

Hot tip

When faced with a really stubborn file, deleting when in Safe Mode is the answer.

A File Opens in the Wrong Program

As an example, you click an image file but instead of opening in the usual imaging program, it opens in a different one.

The reason for this is that another program has installed itself as the default program for opening files of that type. Early versions of Paintshop Pro did this.

The solution is to reinstate your favored program as the default. Do this as follows:

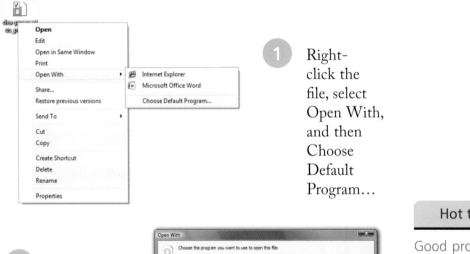

1 Right-click the file, select Open With, and then Choose Default Program…

2 If your desired program is listed, select it. Otherwise click Browse…

Hot tip

Good programs will let the user choose whether or not to make them the default program. The option will be offered during the installation procedure.

...cont'd

 Locate the folder of the program you want and click it to open it

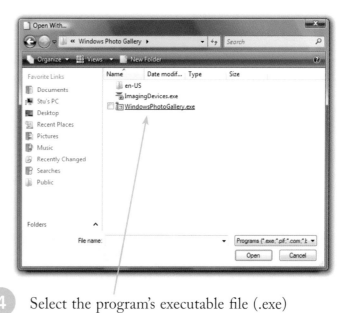

Don't forget

When setting a program as the default, you must select its executable file.

4 Select the program's executable file (.exe)

Your file will now open with the selected program.

A File won't Open

You click a file but it does not open; instead you get an error message. The message will often provide a clue as to the cause of the problem but not always.

The most likely reasons are:

The File is Corrupt (Damaged)
In this situation, unless the file is included in a backup you have previously made, there is nothing you can do to restore it to a working condition. If it has been backed up, though, you will be able to restore it (if you don't know how, just follow the instructions in the backup program's Help file).

Users of Windows Vista have another option. This is the Previous Versions utility – see pages 162–163.

A Compatible Program Isn't Installed on the PC
If a program capable of opening the file isn't installed on the PC, you will get the error message shown below:

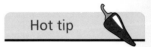

Hot tip

The type of file most likely to be corrupt is video files, particularly those downloaded from the Internet.

157

> Windows cannot open this file:
>
> File: 002.part
>
> To open this file, Windows needs to know what program created it. Windows can go online to look it up automatically, or you can manually select from a list of programs on your computer.
>
> What do you want to do?
>
> ⦿ Use the Web service to find the appropriate program
> ○ Select the program from a list
>
> [OK]   [Cancel]

If you know which program is required, you will have to install it in order to open the file. If you don't, select the first option, "Use the Web service to find the appropriate program". This takes you to a website called cknow (shown on the next page) from where you will be able to identify programs compatible with the file.

...cont'd

The site has a database of all known file types and the programs that can open them. Simply enter the file type of the file that won't open and you will be presented with a list of programs with which the file is compatible.

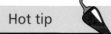
File type   Compatible program

Now all you have to do is acquire the program in order to open your file.

The File is Incompatible with the Program Version

When they create a new version of a program, most software manufacturers ensure that it is compatible with previous versions, i.e. that files created with the earlier versions will open with the new version and vice versa.

However, at some stage in the evolution of a program, due to technical advances, it becomes necessary to abandon support for some of the earliest versions. Incompatibility is the result.

In this situation your only hope is to look for an older version of the program, perhaps one installed on an older PC.

You are Unable to Locate a File

To enable users to find data on their PCs, all versions of Windows provide a search utility. We'll look at the ones provided by Windows Vista and Windows XP.

Windows Vista

Vista's search utility is called Search. This is tightly integrated in the operating system, and thus is instantly accessible from virtually any location. You will find it on the Start Menu and in any Explorer folder.

One of its best features is that it is contextual, i.e. its search is based on the user's current activity, whether it's searching for utilities in the Control Panel, for music files in Windows Media Player or for files and applications in the Start menu.

When doing a search with Vista, you have three ways to go:

First, do a folder search; this is the best option if you already know which folder the file is located in. Simply enter the name of the file in the search box at the top-right of the relevant folder window and the utility will search the folder and display the results of the search. (Note that, by default, the search will be restricted to the contents of the folder, including sub-folders.)

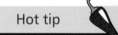

Hot tip

A folder search will only find content that is located in the folder the search is conducted from. Don't use this for a system-wide search.

Folder search box

Second, use the utility's search filters. Do this if you've forgotten the name of the file or have no idea where it is.

159

...cont'd

To access this option, click Search on the Start Menu. This opens the Search utility.

Click Advanced Search and you will see a set of filters. These enable you to search by location (specific drives), date created and size; and while they are unlikely to pinpoint the file, they will produce a narrowed-down list. This should be small enough to search through relatively quickly.

The third way is to use the Start Menu search box. This is the best option if you know the name of the file but have no idea where it is located. This will search the entire computer.

With this option you can locate not only files and folders, but also programs, emails and offline web pages.

Windows XP

XP's Search utility does not provide the folder or Start Menu search options that the one in Windows Vista does.

To access the utility, click Search on the Start menu. On the left-hand side you will see a list of search parameters. Use these to locate your file.

Folder Menu Bars have Disappeared

This issue is specific to Windows Vista. In older versions of Windows, when a folder is opened a menu bar is visible just above the folder's contents.

In Vista, however, this is not the case. As we suspect many users will want this feature, here are two ways to get it back.

The first restores it permanently and is done as follows:

1 Open any folder and click the Organize button

2 Click Layout and then click Menu Bar

3 The menu bar will now be permanently restored on all folders

The second way is to restore it temporarily as and when it is required.

1 Press the Alt key on the keyboard

2 The menu bar will now appear

Note that the Alt key method allows you to make only one selection before the menu bar disappears again. Each time you want to make a selection, you will need to press the Alt key.

Recovering a Deleted File

You've deleted a file, either by accident or design, and now wish to get it back.

Your first option is to check the Recycle Bin (located on the Desktop) – this is a special folder that Windows uses as a cache for all deleted data. All files that you delete will be placed here – they're not actually deleted at all. This gives you a chance to get the file back should you change your mind. Simply open the Recycle Bin, right-click the file and click Restore – it will be restored to its original location.

However, if you have already emptied the Recycle Bin things become much more tricky. It may still be possible to restore the file but this will require the use of a third-party utility.

To understand this, you need to be aware that when a file is deleted its contents will still be on the hard drive until the space they are occupying is overwritten by data subsequently written to the drive. For example, if you delete a file and then immediately create a new one, there is a good chance that the new file will overwrite the deleted one. When this happens, it will be gone for good.

So the first rule when in this situation is not to create any more files or install programs (if you do, you may overwrite the file you wish to recover). You will have to buy a program that is capable of recovering data from the hard drive (Norton System Works is a typical example).

Run the program from the installation disc (don't install it, for the reason already mentioned) and it should be able to recover your file.

Some users of Windows Vista have another option available to them – the Previous Versions utility. Not only can this recover deleted files, it can also restore modified and damaged files to their original state. However, it is not available to users of the Starter, Home Basic and Home Premium editions of Vista.

The application is integrated with the Backup and System Restore utilities, and it uses the data saved in backups and system restore points. For the feature to work, i.e. for previous versions of a file to be available, you must have at least one of the utilities enabled – or both, to get the best results.

In operation it's quite straightforward. In the case of a damaged or modified file that you want to restore, simply right-click the file and click Restore Previous Versions.

Beware

If you restore a file, it will replace the current version. As this action cannot be undone, make sure there's nothing in the current version that you want to keep. If there is, copy it elsewhere first.

Outlook Properties

| General | Shortcut | Security | Details | Previous Versions |

Previous versions come from shadow copies, which are saved automatically to your computer's hard disk, or from backup copies. How do I use previous versions?

File versions:

Name	Date modified	Location
Today (1)		
Outl...	10/10/2007 9:56 AM	Shadow copy
Yesterday (1)		
Outl...	10/10/2007 10:21 ...	Shadow copy
Earlier this month (1)		
Outl...	10/10/2007 10:50 ...	Shadow copy

Open   Copy...   Restore...

OK   Cancel   Apply

You'll see a list of available previous versions of the file. These will either be shadow copies (taken from a system restore point), backup copies (taken from a backup), or both.

To restore a file, select it and then click the Restore button. If it's a backup copy, a Restore Files wizard will open – just follow the prompts. If it's a shadow copy, the file will be restored immediately – this is the quicker of the two options.

In the case of a deleted file that you want to recover, right-click the program with which the file was last opened, or the folder it was located in. Note that a previous version will be available only if a backup or restore point was created prior to the file being deleted.

You've Deleted the Recycle Bin

This issue is specific to Windows Vista only.

Although there is an Empty option within the Recycle Bin folder, a quicker way to empty it is to right-click the folder and click Empty. However, for reasons known best to Microsoft there is also a Delete option on the right-click menu, which if selected (and it's very easy to do it by mistake) will remove the Recycle Bin from the Desktop completely.

We guarantee that virtually all users will do this on occasion, so here's how to get it back when you do it yourself.

1   Right-click the Desktop and click Personalize

2   In the "Personalize appearance and sounds" dialog box, click "Change desktop icons" on the left under Tasks

3   You'll notice that the selection box next to Recycle Bin is unchecked. Check it, click OK and close the dialog box. The Recycle Bin will now be restored to its usual position on the Desktop

14 The Desktop, Taskbar & Start Menu

The Desktop, Taskbar and Start Menu provide entry to your computer. In this chapter we look at typical problems and how to overcome them.

Changing the Wallpaper

You don't like the existing wallpaper and wish to change it to something else: how do you go about it?

With Windows Vista, right-click an empty area of the Desktop and click Personalize. Then click Desktop Background.

Make your selection and click OK

Windows XP users need to right-click an empty area of the Desktop and select Properties. In the dialog box that opens, click the Desktop tab.

From the drop-down box under Background, select a picture and then click Apply

Icons are the Wrong Size

The icons on your PC are either too large (giving a chunky pixelated appearance) or too small (making them difficult to distinguish). To adjust their size, in both Vista and XP, do the following:

 Open the Advanced Appearance dialog box (see top margin note)

 In the drop-down box under Item, select Icon

Hot tip

In Vista, right-click the Desktop and click Personalize. Then click "Window Color and Appearance" and click the Advanced button.

In XP, right-click the Desktop and click Properties. Click the Appearance tab and then the Advanced button.

Advanced Appearance

Inactive Window

Active Window

Normal   Disabled   Selected

Window Text

Message Box   ×

Message Text

OK

Colors and sizes selected here only apply if you have selected a Windows Classic color scheme. If any other scheme is applied, these colors and sizes might not appear.

Item: Size: Color 1:   Color 2:

Icon   32

3D Objects
Active Title Bar
Active Window Border
Application Background
Border Padding
Caption Buttons
Desktop
Disabled Item
Hyperlink
Icon

Size: Color:

9   B I

OK   Cancel

167

Hot tip

If you are running Vista, you can adjust icon size by holding the Ctrl key down and scrolling the mouse wheel – up increases the size and down reduces the size.

In the Size box, select a higher or lower number to adjust the size of the icons accordingly

The "Show Desktop" Icon is Missing

Hot tip

If the Quick Launch toolbar is missing from your Taskbar, right-click the Taskbar and click Toolbars, Quick Launch. You will now see it at the left of the Taskbar.

The Show Desktop icon is found on the Quick Launch toolbar at the left of the Taskbar (if the toolbar isn't there, see top margin note), as shown below:

Show Desktop icon in Windows XP

If, for whatever reason – deletion, corruption, etc – the icon is missing, you can restore it in the way described below.

1. Open a Notepad document (Start, All Programs, Accessories, Notepad)

2. Type the following text into the Notepad document:
   [Shell]
   Command=2
   IconFile=explorer.exe,3
   [Taskbar]
   Command=ToggleDesktop

3. Save the document as "Show Desktop.scf" to the Desktop

4. You will now see a new Show Desktop icon on the Desktop

5. Drag the new icon to the Quick Launch Toolbar

Note that if you are using Windows Vista the procedure above will show the Show Desktop icon that is used with Windows XP. However, it works just the same.

Beware

In step two you must type the text exactly as it appears here.

Hot tip

A quick keyboard shortcut for showing the Desktop is the Windows key +D.

The Volume Control is Missing

This problem is specific to Windows XP. By default, XP does not place the volume control in the Notification Area (its normal location). So if you want to be able to access the control from the Desktop, or it is missing for some reason, you can put it there yourself as follows:

 Go to Start, Control Panel, Sounds and Audio Devices

Sounds and Audio Devices Properties ? X

| Volume | Sounds | Audio | Voice | Hardware |

Sound Blaster 16

Device volume

Low   High

☐ Mute

☑ Place volume icon in the taskbar

Advanced...

Speaker settings

Use the settings below to change individual speaker volume and other settings.

Speaker Volume...   Advanced...

OK   Cancel   Apply

Hot tip

Windows Vista places the volume control in the Notification Area by default. However, if it isn't there for some reason, right-click the Taskbar and click Properties. Then click the Notification Area tab and check the Volume checkbox.

169

On the Volume tab, check the "Place volume icon in the taskbar" checkbox

The volume control will now be accessible from the Notification Area

Quick Launch Applications

The Quick Launch toolbar is very handy for quickly accessing commonly used applications. However, by default it is allocated a limited amount of Taskbar space (typically, enough for three icons), and when this has been used you have to click the chevrons at the right to access the other applications it holds.

Should you wish to have all your Quick Launch applications instantly accessible, resize the toolbar as follows:

1 Right-click the Taskbar and deselect the "Lock the Taskbar" option

2 On either side of the toolbar you will now see "grab handles"

Grab handles

3 Position the mouse pointer over the handle at the right and, when the pointer changes to a double-ended arrow, drag the handle to the right as far as necessary to reveal all your application icons. Then release it

All your application icons are now accessible

4 Right-click the Taskbar and reselect the "Lock the Taskbar" option

The PC's Clock is Wrong

If your PC's clock in the Notification Area of the Taskbar is not showing the correct time, you can reset it in two ways:

The first way is to do it manually. The procedure below shows how it's done with Windows Vista (the procedure with Windows XP is very similar).

1 Click the clock in the Notification Area to open the Date and Time dialog box. Then click "Change date and time settings..."

2 Click "Change date and time..."

Hot tip

If your PC's clock is constantly losing time the cause will be a failing battery. The battery is located on the motherboard and can be replaced.

Date and Time Settings

Set the date and time:

Date:

◄ May 2007 ►

Mo	Tu	We	Th	Fr	Sa	Su
30	1	2	3	4	5	6
7	8	9	10	11	12	13
14	15	16	17	18	19	20
21	22	23	24	25	26	27
28	29	30	31	1	2	3
4	5	6	7	8	9	10

Time:

14:11:13

OK   Cancel

3 Highlight the hour, minutes (as above) or seconds and simply type in the correct figures. Alternatively, use the arrows at the right of the box

The second way is to use the automatic Internet Time utility provided by both XP and Vista. Note that this is enabled by default and, assuming you have a broadband connection, will keep your system clock set accurately.

However, if you don't have a broadband connection you will have to do it manually. Log on to the Internet and then in the Date and Time dialog box (see step one above) click the Internet Time tab. Then click Update Now.

Hot tip

To keep your system's clock automatically updated via the Internet you will need a broadband connection.

How to Configure the Start Menu

The Start Menu is the gateway to your computer and is a highly configurable part of the operating system.

To see what options are available right-click at the top or bottom of the Start Menu and click Properties. Then click Customize.

We won't go through all the options here but, amongst other things, you'll be able to specify which applications appear on the Start Menu and whether they appear as links or menus.

You'll also find customizing options for the Taskbar and the Notification Area.

15 Miscellaneous

This chapter is devoted to a miscellaneous selection of problems that are specific to Windows Vista and Windows XP, and also explains how you can make your PC easier for you to use.

Desktop Spam Messages

A problem that is peculiar to Windows XP is that of unsolicited spam messages periodically popping up on the Desktop.

These messages (an example is shown left) are transmitted via XP's Messenger Service and to get rid of them this service must be disabled.

Do it as follows:

1 Go to Start, Control Panel, Administrative Tools. Then click Services. Locate the Messenger Service and double-click it

2 Stop the Service by clicking Stop

3 In Messenger Properties, select Disabled

Driver Warning Messages

You install a program or new hardware device and up pops a driver warning message, as shown below. Is this something to worry about?

In the majority of cases, it isn't. Ignoring the warning and installing the program regardless will probably have no harmful effect. However, you should be aware that in certain cases it can, hence the warning. For example, if the driver in question is incompatible with the operating system it may cause system instability, lock-ups and crashes.

In an attempt to prevent this, all drivers designed for use with Windows XP and Windows Vista should be approved by Microsoft and given an electronic signature. Any driver that doesn't have this signature will, when installed, invoke an unsigned driver warning message.

When you see one of these messages, cancel the installation and then go to the program or device manufacturer's website and look for a driver certified for use with your operating system. In most cases, one will be available.

However, if one isn't and you really want to install the program or device, do so – but before you do, make sure System Restore is enabled. This will allow you to undo the change should there be any subsequent problems.

Beware

Whether or not you take heed of driver warning messages is entirely up to you. In the vast majority of cases, the driver concerned will be perfectly good.

However, if you install a bad one you could be introducing system instability and other related problems to your PC.

The only way to be absolutely certain that a driver is fully compatible with Windows is to use one that doesn't invoke the warning message.

A Program has Stopped Responding

If you haven't saved your data, closing a non-responding application with the Task Manager may result in you losing that data.

You close a program but instead of disappearing gracefully and without fuss, it insists on hanging around. You click the red X button repeatedly but it refuses to go.

When this happens, after a few moments a dialog box will open asking whether you want to wait until the program closes or to close it yourself. The latter option will usually do the trick; however, it doesn't always work.

In this situation, try the following:

1 Right-click the Taskbar and click Task Manager

Every now and again, you will open a web page that causes your browser to stop responding. Use this procedure to close it.

176

2 Click the Applications tab and you will see the non-responding program. Select it and then click End Task

If you can't close a program even with the Task Manager then it is well and truly frozen. Your only recourse in this situation is to reboot the computer.

3 If even this doesn't work, right-click the program and click Go To Process. Then click the End Process button

Windows Explorer has Crashed

From time to time Windows Explorer, which is the application responsible for the Taskbar, Desktop and Start Menu, will crash. The result is that the Taskbar and all the Desktop icons will disappear leaving a blank screen. With nothing to click, the user seemingly has no options with which to recover.

Don't forget

To open the Task Manager when you have no access to the Taskbar, press Ctrl+Shift+Esc.

The solution is simple:

 Press Ctrl+Shift+Esc. This opens the Task Manager

 From the File menu, click New Task (Run...)

In the Open box, type explorer and then click OK

Windows will now restart Windows Explorer, which will in turn reinstate the Taskbar, Start Menu and Desktop.

Text is Difficult to Read

If you have trouble in reading the text displayed on your monitor although the PC's display system is working (see pages 76–82), you have several options available:

ClearType

If the problem is not too bad and you just need a slight change to improve text clarity sufficiently, ClearType may be all that's required.

This is a feature introduced with Windows XP and continued with Vista, and is an anti-aliasing technique that smooths the edges of fonts, thus making them easier to read. Although intended primarily for LCD monitors, it also makes a noticeable difference when used with a CRT monitor. This is demonstrated clearly with the two samples of text below:

Hot tip

ClearType is more effective on LCD monitors. However, it does improve text clarity on CRT monitors as well, although to a lesser degree.

The popularity of laptops are eager to use mobile XP Professional is designed computing easier. New

The popularity of laptops are eager to use mobile XP Professional is designed computing easier. New

ClearType enabled

ClearType not enabled

To enable ClearType on an XP PC, fire up your browser and go to www.microsoft.com/windowsxp/downloads/powertoys/xppowertoys.mspx. Here you will find the ClearType tuner powertoy. Download and install it on your PC.

Vista users will find the ClearType utility in the Control Panel.

ClearType Settings Wizard

ClearType Tuning

Select the text sample that looks best to you, and then click Next.

| The Quick Brown Fox Jumps Over the Lazy Dog. Lorem ipsum dolor sit amet, consectetuer adipiscing elit, sed deim nonummy nibh euismod tincidunt up lacreet dolore magna aliguam | The Quick Brown Fox Jumps Over the Lazy Dog. Lorem ipsum dolor sit amet, consectetuer adipiscing elit, sed deim nonummy nibh euismod tincidunt up lacreet dolore magna aliguam | The Quick Brown Fox Jumps Over the Lazy Dog. Lorem ipsum dolor sit amet, consectetuer adipiscing elit, sed deim nonummy nibh euismod tincidunt up lacreet dolore magna aliguam |
| The Quick Brown Fox Jumps Over the Lazy Dog. Lorem ipsum dolor sit amet, consectetuer adipiscing elit, sed deim nonummy nibh euismod tincidunt up lacreet dolore magna aliguam | The Quick Brown Fox Jumps Over the Lazy Dog. Lorem ipsum dolor sit amet, consectetuer adipiscing elit, sed deim nonummy nibh euismod tincidunt up lacreet dolore magna aliguam | The Quick Brown Fox Jumps Over the Lazy Dog. Lorem ipsum dolor sit amet, consectetuer adipiscing elit, sed deim nonummy nibh euismod tincidunt up lacreet dolore magna aliguam |

< Back   Next >   Cancel

Windows Magnifier

This works in the same way as a magnifying glass and can be used in several ways. For example: you can set it to track the mouse pointer automatically or to follow the keyboard's focus, or you can move it around yourself to areas that need magnification.

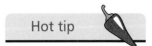
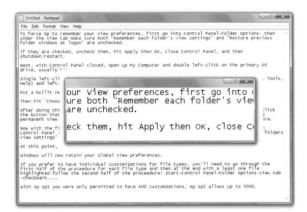

While we wouldn't recommend Windows Magnifier as a permanent solution for those who have trouble reading text on their PCs, it can be handy in some situations.

In Windows XP you can access the utility in the Control Panel by clicking "Accessibility Options", and in Windows Vista you can do it by clicking "Ease of Access Center".

Click Start Magnifier

Resolution

If neither ClearType nor Windows Magnifier provides an adequate solution, the next option is to reduce the PC's resolution. This will increase the size of everything: icons, text and windows.

1 If you are running Windows XP, right-click the Desktop and click Properties. Then click the Settings tab. Vista users should right-click the Desktop and click Personalization. Then click Display Settings

2 Drag the slider back to select a lower resolution and click OK

3 A dialog box will appear asking whether you want to keep the new setting; click Yes

You may need to experiment with the different resolutions until you find the one that's best for you.

Windows Narrator

If you are unable to read what's on the screen even at the lowest resolution (800 x 600), your only option is to use a screen reader (text to speech). These are available as commercial products but both Windows XP and Vista provide a basic reader called Narrator.

This utility provides the following options:

● Reads the contents of the active window and menu options

● Reads typed characters

● Moves the mouse pointer to the active item

Beware

Windows Narrator is designed to work with Notepad, WordPad, Control Panel programs, Internet Explorer, the Windows Desktop, and some parts of Windows Setup. It may not read words aloud correctly in other programs.

181

In Windows XP you can access Narrator by going to Start, All Programs, Accessories, Accessibility. In Windows Vista go to Start, All Programs, Accessories, Ease of Access.

Note that Narrator is not suitable for continuous use. If the only way you can use your PC is with the aid of a screen reader, you will have to buy a more proficient program of this type.

Sounds are Difficult to Hear

If you have trouble hearing the sounds produced by your PC, the most obvious solution is to increase the volume. If there is a volume control on the speakers, set it to a higher level.

If this control has already been set as high as possible, or there isn't one available on the speakers, you will need to adjust the system's volume control.

Look at the Notification Area at the far right of the Taskbar and you should see a volume control. If there isn't one there, refer to page 85 where we explain how to make it appear in the Notification Area.

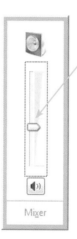

Click the volume control's icon to open it and then simply drag the slider up to increase the PC's volume level.

If you double-click the icon, a more fully featured dialog box (shown below) will open, which gives you more options.

If you still can't hear the PC's sounds even at the highest volume setting and the PC's sound system is working (see page 83), your only alternative is to use text or visual alerts as a substitute for sound. You will find the option to set this up in the "Ease of Access" utility (Windows Vista) and "Accessibility Options" (Windows XP) in the Control Panel.

The Mouse is Difficult to Use

People with hand or wrist disabilities can find a standard mouse difficult to use. Fortunately, there are alternatives.

Use the Keyboard as a Mouse

Go to "Accessibility Options" (Windows Vista) or "Ease of Access" (Windows XP) in the Control Panel and you will be able to access a utility known as Mouse Keys.

This enables you to control the mouse pointer with the keyboard's numeric keypad (the numbered keys at the right-hand side). The 1,7,9 and 3 keys move the pointer diagonally; the 4 and 5 keys move it left and right; and the 8 and 2 keys move it up and down.

Trackball Mouse

This device is essentially an upturned ball and wheel mouse. Instead of the ball making contact with the desk, the user moves it with a finger or palm. Thus it requires less physical movement from the user, and so is much easier to operate.

There are many different types of trackball mouse available, for example devices that incorporate a multiway joystick and ones that use a touchpad (shown left). These can be operated with no hand or wrist movement.

Hands-Free Devices

For users who are unable to operate any kind of mouse at all, there is a device known as SmartNAV. It is operated by small head movements using an adhesive reflective dot worn on the user's forehead or glasses. This movement is picked up by a sensor clipped to the monitor and converted into mouse pointer movement.

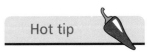

Hot tip

You can toggle the Mouse Keys on and off by pressing ALT + SHIFT + NUMLOCK.

Beware

The more specialized mice tend to be much more expensive than standard models.

The Keyboard is Difficult to Use

As with the mouse, there is a range of keyboards designed for users who have difficulty operating standard models.

Large Key Keyboards
At the basic level we have keyboards with keys up to four times larger than standard keys. The keys may also be brightly colored to aid those who are visually impaired.

Keyless Keyboards
These devices, such as the OrbiTouch shown right, replace all the keys with two domes.

You type the different characters by sliding the domes to create letters and numbers.
(This particular model also has an integrated mouse, so moving the domes gives you full mouse and keyboard capabilities.)

On-Screen Keyboards
These are software-generated keyboards that appear on the screen and are operated with the mouse and, in some cases, by using switches.

These programs are available commercially or you can try the one provided by Windows (shown below).

In Windows Vista you can access the on-screen keyboard by going to Start, All Programs, Accessories, Ease of Access. In Windows XP go to Start, All Programs, Accessories, Accessibility.

Hot tip

Some on-screen keyboards will allow pictures and graphics to be placed on the screen, which can send associated words, phrases, pictures or commands to the program being used.
For example, a picture of a house could send an address to a word processor.

Easy Calculating

The calculator provided by Windows is a very handy and much-used application. However, operating it with a mouse can be difficult for the physically impaired, and it is very easy to press the wrong button. You could never add up a column of figures with it at anything like the speed at which you could do it with a real calculator.

Try using it a different way:

1 Press the Num Lock key on the keyboard

2 Open the calculator by going to Start, All Programs, Accessories, Calculator

Don't forget

The calculator can be expanded to a scientific mode. Select this option from the View menu.

3 Instead of fiddling about with the mouse to enter numbers, simply use the numeric keypad on the keyboard, together with the keys shown in this table:

Hot tip

While the calculator supplied by Windows is perfectly adequate for most needs, there is a range of far superior and specialized calculators available for download from the Internet.

Key	Action
/	The equivalent of divide
*	The equivalent of multiply
+	The equivalent of plus
-	The equivalent of minus
Enter	The equivalent of equals

Windows won't Log on Automatically

This problem is specific to Windows XP. Every time you start your XP PC, instead of Windows going straight to the Desktop it stops with a log on dialog box, as shown in the screenshot below.

186

1 To get to the Desktop you have to enter a password and then click OK

Should you not require this or find it a nuisance, you can get rid of the log on box as follows:

2 Go to Start, Control Panel, User Accounts. Click "Change the way users log on or off"

3 Uncheck the "Use the Welcome screen" checkbox

However, if you have more than one account, Windows will still stop at the Welcome screen, this time showing a list of the accounts. To access the Desktop you have to select one of them, so you're still not being logged on automatically.

The solution here is to delete all but one of the accounts. To do this, open User Accounts as described in step two but this time click "Change an Account". Select the relevant accounts in turn and click "Delete this account".

Index